Women's Soccer
Techniques, Tactics & Teamwork

Robert "Butch" Lauffer

U.S.S.F. National Staff Coach and
Head Coach, Men's and Women's Soccer
West Texas A&M University

April Kater

Head Coach, Women's Soccer
Syracuse University

Sterling Publishing Co., Inc.
New York

Photos printed with permission and through the courtesy of:
University of Notre Dame Soccer (photographer Pete LaFleur): page 106.
Rutgers University Soccer (photographer Larry Levanti): pages 37, 92.
Nebraska University Soccer (photographer Matt Miller): pages 1, 5, 64, 71, 87, 129.
West Texas A&M University Soccer (photographer Mike Jones): pages 44, 49, 77, 82, 96.
All other photographs, Syracuse University Soccer (photographer Steve Parker)
    and its players.

Artist: Marc Eisenburg
Photographer: Steve Parker
Typist: Connie Villescas
Editor: Claire Bazinet

Library of Congress Cataloging-in-Publication Data
Lauffer, Robert.
    Women's Soccer; techniques, tactics & teamwork / Robert "Butch" Lauffer
& April Kater.
        p. cm.
    Includes index.
    ISBN 0-8069-5847-2
    1. Soccer for women—Juvenile literature. [1. Soccer for women.]
    I. Kater, April. II. Title

    GV944.5 .L38 2001
    796.334'2—dc21   00-048258

10 9 8 7 6 5 4 3 2 1

Published by Sterling Publishing Company, Inc.
387 Park Avenue South, New York, N.Y. 10016
© 2001 by Robert "Butch" Lauffer and April Kater
Distributed in Canada by Sterling Publishing
C/o Canadian Manda Group, One Atlantic Avenue, Suite 105
Toronto, Ontario, Canada M6K 3E7
Distributed in Great Britain and Europe by Cassell PLC
Wellington House, 125 Strand, London WC2R 0BB, England
Distributed in Australia by Capricorn Link (Australia) Pty Ltd.
P.O. Box 6651, Baulkham Hills, Business Centre, NSW 2153, Australia
Printed in China

Sterling ISBN 0-8069-5847-2

Acknowledgments

I would like to take this opportunity to say "thank you" to all the people who helped me, and made this book possible.

To all the players and coaches I have had the pleasure of working with over twenty years of coaching.

To my staff at West Texas A&M University, Charlie Hatfield, Chad Webb, and Lee Hanvey, for all their support, friendship, and their feedback on the book while it was in progress.

To great friends Randy Waldrun, Head Coach of Notre Dame, and Felix Oskan, Head Coach of Texas Tech University, for their feedback as well.

To my lovely wife, Kim, without whose support this work would never have been finished…and whom I love very much.

To Kendall and Blake for their undivided love.

And to my Dad, who taught me to be the best I could be.

Butch Lauffer

I am grateful to Butch Lauffer for asking me to co-author this book. He has so much knowledge about the sport of soccer and having the opportunity to contribute my thoughts and ideas to his is a privilege. Special thanks to Randy Waldrum for investing his time and sharing his opinions with our readers. Having Randy endorse our work is an honor.

I would like to thank Maren Rojas, for allowing me to use her drills and expertise in the goalkeeping chapter. To all the players who helped with the photographs: Whitney Cali, Erika Hadjoglou, Kim Kisner, Robyn Malloy, Maren Rojas, Ashley Riggs, and Riley Wogamon. To Steve Parker, who truly is one of the best photographers in the wide world of sport.

My personal thanks to all the coaches who have shared with me their knowledge and passion for the game of soccer. To all the players I have coached, thank you for allowing me to do the same.

I would like to dedicate this book to my parents, for taking me to my first soccer game, and to hundreds more thereafter.

April Kater

Foreword

Randy Waldrum
Head Coach, Women's Soccer,
University of Notre Dame

Endorsing coaching philosophy or styles is often risky, since there are so many different ways of achieving success in this game. However, endorsing coaches whom I've come to know over the years is something much easier for me to do, since we all come to respect certain people in our particular profession. The authors of this book, April Kater and Butch Lauffer, are truly two of our country's best coaches. I found that this coaching manual contained many activities that I not only agree with, but that we incorporate here at the University of Notre Dame. I also found it concise, easy to understand, and that the progressions of each practice makes very logical sense. As coaches, these are the things we look for when trying to further our knowledge of the game.

I had the good fortune many years ago to be an instructor at a U.S. Soccer National Coaching Course where April Kater was a candidate. She not only was the top female candidate, but was one of the top candidates in the entire course. I now get the good fortune of competing against her as her team, Syracuse University, competes against us in the Big East Conference. Her teams are always good, competitive, and play with imagination, which is what I personally love to see. I believe, at this time in the evolution of the women's game, where we are starting to develop a generation of top female coaches, April is one of the best in the country.

As for Coach Lauffer, I really don't know where to start. Butch is without a doubt one of the best coaches we have at this time. His knowledge and experience are great resources for all of us coaching out there. Not only does he have an extended amount of experience coaching youth, college, and national teams, but he also has some tremendous amounts of insight into international football. I also must admit that Butch is one of my very best friends. As a member of U.S. Soccer's National Coaching Staff, Butch is also privy to current trends in the game today. He runs a very successful men and women's program at West Texas A&M University, and somehow, in between all of this, has found the time to help many coaches around the country get exposure coaching internationally through his "International Coaching Course," which he hosts each spring.

As a coach in the women's game and as an advocate of the growth of women's athletics in general, I am really happy to see this book, addressing the women's game. I do believe that, though the x's and o's may be the same, there are some differences in comparing the women's game to the men's. I am sure, though, that you will find that the information covered in this book will be insightful, useful, and will open your mind to some new ideas about the game. April and Butch give it a unique "touch," if you will, as both offer their own perspectives and ideas—insights from a male and a female coach's vantage point.

Our thanks and appreciation go out to you both for taking the time out of your extremely busy schedules to write this wonderful guide to coaching women's soccer.

Contents

Preface, or Coaching by the Difference

In general, playing soccer and taking part in other such sports activities is beneficial to players, regardless of sex, in many ways, including:

self-esteem • discipline • teamwork • leadership • handling competition • recognition • motivation • general health and well-being • learning perseverance • winning with class • losing with grace • trust

The proper development of soccer skills depends generally on three areas: each player's overall athletic ability, the repetition of training programs to develop skills, and the quality of feedback and reinforcement each player receives from his or her coach. In my years of coaching both women's and men's soccer, I've learned that the difference isn't in the kinds of instruction given. Women and men process information in the same way, so they can learn the same formations, or systems, and standards of play. Certain systems, however, might be better suited for women, or for men, based on physical ability, or due to other differences or limitations relating to the individual players themselves. The difference is largely in how soccer instruction is presented or verbalized.

In coaching women as opposed to men, I've learned to approach women players from a psychological standpoint. The female athlete, in general, is motivated differently than the male athlete. There are behavior ranges within both genders, but men overall, for example, tend to value independence, self-confidence, the freedom to challenge authority, individual and external competition, and the success their status brings. Women value cohesiveness, intimacy, interdependence, and emotions. Men tend to fear dependence and failure, while women tend to fear isolation and separation.

Women as a whole don't want to be singled out from the team, whether for praise or correction. Doing so can have a negative effect, largely because of the women's desire to be liked and to feel a part of the team. They want to connect and maintain relationships with their teammates, and their coaches, even while performing as competitive athletes. In team discussions, they will often suppress their own true feelings and concerns in order to keep the peace, or the approval of their coach and teammates.

Where men will immediately respond with questions and challenge authority, female players tend to accept instructions as stated. They also interpret them more literally than men do. This is a problem in that the game of soccer is made up largely of gray areas, not black-and-white situations. A player who is not sure what is expected may fail to follow through on an instruction due to a fleeting "moment of hesitation." This comes from the women's drive for approval and wish to please. To overcome this reluctance to speak out, women athletes should be encouraged to do so. They need to know that their coach cares about them. Once they have learned to trust you as their coach, and know that you want to develop them into the best soccer players they can be, they will run through a brick wall for you!

Cross-gender coaching is quite common in women's soccer as in other sports. Among themselves, as do men or boys, women or girl athletes can be quite open, not necessarily having to do with sports. They may also not realize, or care, that you are within earshot. Long boring bus or van rides to games can allow you to get the pulse of the team or individuals, as well as to schedule some study for yourself.

One situation that I've observed numerous times is that male coaches who are coaching women often fail to hold their female athletes up to the same standard they would players on a men's team. This is a huge mistake! Women want to be challenged, and they are quick to figure out if you, as a coach, are not doing your job. The attitude I take in coaching women, as well as men, is that I know what it takes to win. I also train my women's team as "soccer players," not as female soccer players. I tell my women players that, until they show me different, I'll treat them like soccer players on the field, and like "ladies" off the field.

As a coach of women's soccer, it is in your best interest to try to find out what establishes each player's self-worth. You can do this by improvised or scheduled meetings. The knowledge will be very useful in motivating that player, and raising her self-esteem and confidence. Consider how you talk to your players before, during, and after training and games. Your tone and vocabulary are critical in promoting each player's and the team's self-worth and getting them to play their best. You cannot yell at your woman players all the time, as you may tend to do with their male counterparts at training and at the games. They do not respond to it, and will quickly shut you off. Instead, in order to get the team to respond with more fire, a firm talking-to at halftime during a game can work miracles. Communication works! This past year at West Texas A&M, we were struggling with injuries and a losing streak that this group of players had never experienced. The night before the game, I decided to play low-pressure, and play on the break. After a longer than normal pregame team meeting, the women went out, executed the game plan to perfection, and we won 1–0! If you've taught them well and they are "with you," they will do everything not to let you down.

Butch Lauffer

1

Technique

DRIBBLING

Dribbling is the ability of a player to move the ball at a reasonable pace, keeping it close to the feet, under pressure from an opponent. Dribbling is one of the most exciting parts of the game of soccer. It's a player's way of self-expression during play. As soccer has matured, adding ever more sophisticated defensive systems, coaches have had to develop players who have the mentality, technical ability, and awareness of how and when to take players on. A player with good dribbling skills can destroy the best organized defense in the world. Advanced levels of play demand that all players on a team, including defenders, develop equally strong skills in dribbling with either foot.

Principles of Dribbling

Vision See the field in between ball touches. Be alert to teammates and opponents, as well as to the opening and closing of spaces.

Close Control Be efficient in using all parts of the foot (inside, outside, sole) and both feet equally when dribbling.

Balance   Keep a low center of gravity (bend knees) to be able to stop, start, and accelerate quickly. To dribble well, a player must be able to stay on her feet, and to concentrate even when being tackled or pressured by an opponent.

Agility   An ability to beat opponents, using quick, sharp changes of direction and cutbacks.

Change of Pace   To change direction and beat an opponent 1 v 1, a player should use different speeds: accelerating as the ball is pushed past a defender or cutting the ball back to escape pressure.

Feints   Use the body as well as the ball to manipulate an opponent off balance.

Attitude   Have the courage and willingness to dribble at opponents. This attitude will increase goal-scoring chances for the player and the team. It also may provide great dividends in the form of free kicks.

Common Faults

- Head down
- Dribbling with toe
- Ball too far away
- Upright stance
- No change of pace or direction
- Flat-footed, no balance
- Bad decisions on when/where to dribble

Dribbling Techniques

Attacking Space   When attacking space, a player should take less touches, pushing the ball farther ahead to comfortably run at full speed. In this way, the player creates enough time to look up and recognize any opportunities arising in front of her while she covers as much ground as quickly as possible. Players tend to use the outside of their feet when executing this technique.

dribbling

1

2

3

shielding/turning

Attacking a Defender When attacking a defender, tighter, more controlled touches are needed. The coach should work on encouraging players in this situation to recognize and attack the front foot of the defender. This will unbalance them. A player can also dribble at a defender to create space for someone else to run into.

Players need to be able to use all parts of their feet, and both feet equally, when dribbling under pressure. It is much easier for an opponent to defend against a player who is predominantly one-sided. It's also important for the coach to create a training environment that will encourage proper decision-making regarding when and when not to dribble.

Attacking away from Defender (shielding)
Players often find themselves in situations where their primary goal is to maintain ball possession, rather than penetrate. This can occur anywhere on the field; thus every player must be able to shield the ball.

By using a sideways-on stance, a player can create a large barrier between the ball and a defender. It is also the best way for a player to keep her balance while being physically pressured by a defender. The ball should be on the foot farthest from the defender, and the player should be constantly looking up to evaluate opportunities to release the ball to a teammate, or to spin off of the defender and continue dribbling away from pressure.

Practices—Attacking Defenders

Warm-Up Players each maneuver a ball in a 20-by-20-yard grid, practicing change of pace and direction using various surfaces of each foot. The coach may add restrictions; for example, left foot only for one minute.

Individual 1 v 1 to cones, unlimited space. The attacker must beat the defender on the dribble and hit the cone with the ball to score. One-minute games, winners move up one cone, while the losers move down one cone. Encourage the player to be explosive and change pace when beating the defender.

warm-up

attacking defenders, small group

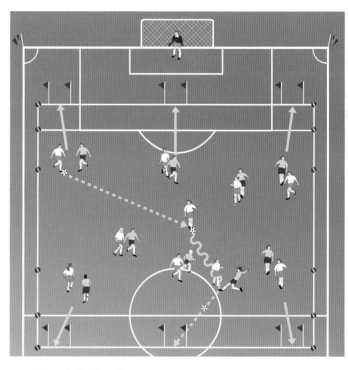

attacking defenders, large group

Small Group   4 v 4 to big goals with goalkeepers, 30-by-40-yard field. The coach should look to help the player in making decision when, when not, to dribble. Play five-minute games. Winning team stays on, losing team comes off to do some type of active rest.

Large Group   9 v 9 to 3 or more goals. Attacking team tries to dribble across the end line to score.

Game   11 v 11 to big goals with goalkeepers, regulation-size field. Attacking team tries to score through the regular run of the game. However, stress 1 v 1 opportunities and promote risk-taking in the attacking third.

PASSING

Passing is the ability to strike the ball over a distance and successfully find a teammate or enough space to maintain possession. Some passes are as short as five yards; others can be as long as a 60-yard serve in the air. Regardless of distance or purpose, a pass is successful only if it reaches your teammate.

When it comes to passing, the coach needs to work with the players to understand the techniques of passing and how the priorities of passing are interrelated. They are: 1) penetration, to feet or to space, 2) changing the point of attack, and 3) a back or possession pass.

TRAINING AREA GUIDELINES

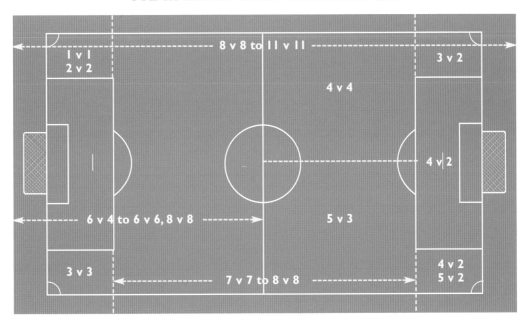

For practices and training activities, there are times when you will want to limit space, and perhaps have several groups of players practice separately. This diagram is provided to serve as a guide to such allocation of space, to be adjusted as needed for various activities.

Principles of Passing

Accuracy The passer must decide when to play to feet or into space in front of a teammate. Often this is dictated by the open player asking for the ball and not by the passer. The passer needs to be able to read and anticipate teammate runs in order to make the right decision.

Weight Playing a pass too strongly can cause the ball to be missed or uncontrollable; a pass without enough pace can result in an interception.

Timing The passer must release the ball at the appropriate time. This can be helped by working with your players on three simple concepts:

1) "head up," the head of the player in possession comes up, indicating she is ready to pass the ball; 2) "show," the player inviting the pass shows she's ready for a possible pass; and 3) "pass," the pass is made and completed.

Disguise Passer must try to conceal her intention from the opponent. Avoid being obvious when passing the ball.

Common Faults
- Choosing wrong part of foot to pass the ball
- Incorrect approach angle
- Failure to keep eyes on ball
- Non-kicking foot too far from ball
- Incorrect follow-through
- Ankle unlocked
- Head comes up too early

Passing Techniques

Push Pass Kicking the soccer ball with the inside of the foot is the most accurate method of passing. It is also the easiest passing method a soccer player will learn. The approach of the player to the ball should always be in a straight line behind the ball, not at an angle, where a player can lose balance and accuracy. The "push pass" should be used mainly over shorter distances because the majority of the power is coming only from the leg striking the ball and not from the entire body. Often players become too comfortable using the inside of the foot to push pass and try to serve balls over longer distances, on the ground or even in the air, and they are unsuccessful.

Instep Drive Kicking "with the laces" is the most powerful method of passing a ball. When using the instep, a player is attempting to pass the ball over longer distances. Here, though, the most common

instep drive

1

2

3

4

outside-the-foot pass

mistakes at all levels come into play: toes not pointed down and/or ankle not locked. The approach should also be slightly angled, allowing the player a full backswing. In addition, the height of the kick will be determined by the player's moving the upper body forward, over the ball. Defenders will often use the instep pass when bypassing the midfield to connect with their forwards. Midfielders will use the instep pass to change the point of attack with a long powerful pass from one flank to the other. Forwards can use the instep drive when shooting on goal.

Swerve Pass Although using the same surface of the foot as when executing the push pass, bending a ball with the inside of the foot can be a more challenging technique to complete. The swerve pass can be used over medium to long distances and a ball can be bent around defenders to a team-mate. The angle of approach is similar to the push pass; however one must strike the ball slightly off-center, and the upper body must lean back if a player intends to elevate the pass. Defenders and midfielders should be the most proficient in using the swerve pass.

Outside-the-Foot Pass Probably the most difficult pass to master, the outside-the-foot pass is the most unpredictable to defend against. The approach should be straight or slightly angled, depending on the intended spin effect. When the ball is struck, the kicking foot should be pointed down and angled towards the inside of the player, with the ankle locked. The most important factor is that the ball must be struck off-center to make the ball bend. The outside-the-foot pass can be used over any distance—short deceptive passes to long services behind the defense. Players will also use the outside-the-foot technique when taking free kicks, the spin created can manipulate a ball around a wall.

laces lofted pass

Technique

Lofted Pass   The lofted pass is a skill used in many aspects of the game of soccer. Goalkeepers or defenders use it when taking goal kicks; defenders, on occasion, when clearing a ball out of a danger area. Attackers will use it when crossing a ball, and it also can be used when taking free kicks. The priority is height; therefore, the player's body position should be leaning away and back from the ball. Also, the instep of the foot, "with the laces," should strike the ball through the bottom half, making it rise. The player should also hit through the middle of the ball to avoid pulling or slicing.

Chipping   Unlike other passing techniques, chipping the ball allows for little or no follow-through. The kicking action is a simple "jab" under the bottom half of the ball with the top of the kicking toe. This pass is advantageous over shorter distances because, like the push-pass, little power is generated from the body to the ball. Often, players will use a chip to get over or behind an opponent when other passing alternatives are not available.

Volley   This technique is very common in a game, but quite difficult to master. The full volley is the more popular type of kicking method, where the player kicks the ball before it touches the ground. This technique can be performed in two ways: by approaching either down the line of flight of the ball, or across the line of flight of the ball. In addition, volleying a ball differs technically when comparing a defensive volley to an attacking volley. When defending, you want to clear the ball far, high, and wide. When attacking, you want to be compact and keep the ball low for more power.

chipping game

Inside-the-Foot Volley The approach should be directly down the line of flight of the ball. The kicking action starts with the lifting and opening up of the kicking leg from the hip. The nonkicking foot is pointed towards the target. The knee of the same leg should be slightly bent, providing balance and stability. The final motion is the kicking action, from the knee down of the kicking leg, where the lower leg is stiff. The contact foot should strike the ball through the midline, while the foot is turned at a right angle. The follow-through should be short and towards the target. When shooting the ball, the upper body should be upright and leaning back slightly. Arms should be out to the sides to provide balance and protection. When defending, the ball should be struck underneath the midline and the player should be leaning back much farther, to give the kick height.

When attacking the ball across the line, again the player's kicking foot is pointing towards the target. This allows the player to open up and face the ball down this line of flight. The knee should be raised until the kicking foot is even with the height of the ball. The whole leg is then brought forward across the body while the contact foot strikes the ball through the midline at a right angle. Again, when defending, the difference is not in the technique, but rather in how much the upper body is leaning back and striking underneath the ball.

Instep Volley The approach should be directly down the line of flight of the ball. The nonkicking foot is pointing towards the target and the standing leg is used for balance. As the ball approaches, the knee of the kicking leg is brought up while the contact foot is pointed straight down and locked

inside-the-foot volley

instep volley

at the ankle. The lower leg bends slightly back and then snaps through the ball as the foot strikes, with the laces, through the midline of the ball or slightly above to keep the shot low. The kicking knee should be over the ball as it is struck, helping to keep the shot low and powerful. The upper body should be upright, and arms out for balance and protection. On the defense, two major points of the instep volley are: 1) the knee should *not* be over the ball, and 2) the foot should make contact *below* the midline of the ball. In addition, the player should be leaning back to help ensure that the ball goes high and, hopefully, far.

When attacking the ball across the line using this technique, several things have to change. The player's back should virtually turn towards the goal that is being attacked, as the player plants and pivots on the foot nearest to the goal, pointing it towards the target. The leading shoulder should fall away, allowing the kicking leg to rise high enough to swing the pointing toe away. Once the ball is struck, the player should follow through by landing on the kicking foot. Again, when using this technique to defend, the player should be leaning back farther and striking underneath the ball.

Outside-the-Foot Volley The approach should be directly down the line of flight of the ball. As the ball is struck, the knee of the kicking leg should be brought across the thigh of the nonkicking leg. Contact with the ball should be made from the area of the small toe to midway down the outside of the foot. The foot is turned slightly inward with the toe pointed down and inward. Depending on power needed, the attacker may land on the kicking foot. The body should be upright with one arm coming across the chest as the ball is struck and the other out for balance. The ball should be struck slightly left or right of center at the midline depending on which foot is used. This will allow the ball to swerve, making the shot very unpredictable.

Half Volley   When a player is not quick enough or doesn't anticipate the flight of the ball, the result is a half volley. If a player has time and space to allow the ball to drop, the half volley is the preferable technique. The main differences between a half and a full volley are that the half-volley ball is struck as it contacts the ground. The half volley produces a much lower and faster trajectory, and therefore reaches the target faster. In most cases, the attacker will meet the ball down its line of flight. The player should make contact with the laces of the contact foot and slightly above the midline of the ball. The knees should be bent and over the ball, with the body leaning forward. This will keep the shot very low. The nonkicking foot should be pointed towards the target and alongside the ball. The follow-through is a short snap through the ball.

Practice—Elevating Passing Skills

Warm-Up—Individual   Two groups of five, one ball per group using half the field. The two groups of five intermix, but must play only to players in their own group. Now, add a number sequence to each group—example, 1-2-3—and this number sequence must be followed.

Small Group   Playing 5 v 5 + 2 neutral players, with small goals, three-fourths field. The two neutral players, who are always on offense. The object

is to score on the goals but it is also possible to get one extra point for connecting with a neutral player on a long pass. Focus on possession, using all types of passing and recognizing when to serve long vs. short passes.

Large Group   Play 8 v 8 + 2 neutrals, with large goals on top of each six-yard box. The object is to score on goal while maintaining possession. Incorporate crosses into the attack, bending vs. driven passes. Learn choice of passes and the tactical results and effectiveness of certain passes; for example, when to play to feet, or when to play a through pass.

Practice—Shooting

Warm-Up   Each player has a ball. Four regulation-size goals are set up in a 30-by-30-yard grid. Players dribble in the area and, on command, strike balls into the goal they are facing. Add a change of direction on the coach's command, and strike at the farthest goal. Take away half of the balls. Now, combining with an open player before shooting, players must dribble at speed to the nearest goal and play shots into the corners. Play to the stationary target next to the goalkeeper, who pops the ball into the air for a volley. Vary-up different services so all types of shots are being practiced from various distances.

Small Group 1   Play 5 v 2 to two large goals with goalkeepers. 20-by-18-yard grid. The five offensive players must combine five passes together before being allowed to shoot. The team of five must shoot as quickly as possible once the number has been reached and shoot in the direction you are facing. If a defender intercepts the ball she can shoot immediately at either goal.

shooting practice, small group 1

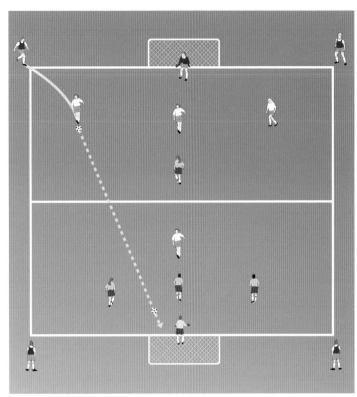

shooting practice, large group

Small Group 2 Play 3 v 1 + 3 v 1. Close game from extended penalty box to big goal with goalkeepers. Shoot whenever possible. Each team goes in one direction and if they score they get the ball back. Once you have scored two goals you stay in and the losing team is off.

Large Group 3 v 1 + 3 v 1 and four servers. Two-penalty-box-size grid. Two teams are separated by the top of the penalty box. Each team plays 3 v 1 in each half. The three try to work themselves free to get a shot in goal. The lone attacker can attack or act as support player to the three and also look for rebounds. If the goalkeeper makes the save, she plays the ball back into play. If the ball goes out of play on either side, the server plays the ball in to one of the three.

HEADING

Heading is the ability to strike the ball with the forehead to score goals, pass, or redirect the ball. Unfortunately, this technique is considered to be one of the weaker points in the women's game. Maybe girls, at a younger age, are cautioned more often than boys are to be careful, so they become afraid to head the ball and compete in the air to win a ball. Another possibility is that some youth coaches don't make heading a priority in their training. Whatever the reason, women wanting to compete at the higher levels of competition must be committed to improving this important aspect of the game.

Principles of Heading

Approach See the ball and adjust the body position according to the flight path of the ball. Get the body as much as possible directly behind the ball.

Accuracy As in any ball technique, it's important to keep the eyes on the ball. This may seem difficult with the ball being struck so close to the eyes.

Timing The power created by the header is a direct result of the snapping motion through the ball. This motion must be done precisely as the ball arrives in front of the body.

Surface The forehead is always used when heading the ball, regardless of the ball being short, redirected, or cleared from a defensive position.

Common Faults

- Jumping off both legs rather than one
- Mistiming the jump; jumping too early or too late
- Failure to watch ball while heading; closing the eyes
- Failure to arch body back, resulting in less power behind the header
- Failure to snap through the ball once struck; lack of follow-through also lessens the power of the header
- Head and neck are not tensed, resulting in an inaccurate header
- Using incorrect surface; e.g., top of the head rather than the forehead

The basic technique of striking a ball with the head should be mastered at a young age; then a player can learn the variations to heading, such as heading from a standing position, heading from a jumping position, and the diving header.

Heading Techniques

Standing Position The feet should be spaced apart, forming a good base, 8–10 inches wide. The feet should also be staggered, to provide balance when the upper body arches backwards as the ball arrives. The trunk of the body should snap forward to give power to the header as the forehead contacts the ball. Point of contact on the ball can vary depending on whether the player is attacking or defending. When heading to score, the contact should be at the midline of the ball, to keep it directed down and low. When defending, the contact should be made below the midline of the ball, with the upper body continuing forward in the snapping motion.

standing header

one-footed-jump header

One-Footed Take-Off   The player should be sure that, when jumping off one leg, she chooses the leg most appropriate to the situation. Some players prefer jumping off of one leg over the other; therefore, a coach should make sure players are able to jump off of either leg successfully when attempting to head the ball. On takeoff, the knee and ankle of the takeoff leg should push upward and should arch backwards after the jump. The action of the non-takeoff leg should swing forward and high, bending at the hip and knee. The upper body should be leaning forward at the point of takeoff and, when maximum height is reached, the body should arch backwards. The momentum of reaching back in a snapping motion propels the upper body forward, and the energy generated puts power behind the header. The head and neck should be tense as the forehead meets the ball. The player should end up landing on both feet.

Two-Footed Take-Off   The player should start from a staggered or parallel standing position. The arms should be swung backwards and the knees slightly bent with the upper body leaning forward. The arms should then swing forward as the legs straighten out and the feet push off the ground. The upper body then leans backwards and snaps forward as the forehead meets the ball. The player should end up landing on both feet.

To Redirect Ball   The player's jumping should be rotated towards the intended direction so that the surface of the forehead and the upper body are at the right angle to redirect the ball. In addition, when heading from a jump-and-turning action, it is best to jump with the leg that is closest to the ball. The opposite leg must then swing in the direction of the ball, in order to help rotate the trunk.

Diving Header   There are instances when a ball is served below head height, but still too high to successfully strike with the foot. As one foot pushes off the ground, the opposite leg kicks in an upward motion while the upper body leans forward and arms are extended forward. The body is parallel to the ground as the forehead strikes the midline of the ball. Arms are still extended outward to help brace the landing as the body connects with the ground at roughly a 45-degree angle.

two-footed-jump header

diving header

Practice—Heading to Score and Defend

Warm-Up Team handball, players can pass with their hands but can only score using their head. Make sure all the players give special attention to stretching neck muscles, torso, and back before a session on heading.

Individual Groups of 3, two servers 15 yards apart, one player working in the middle. Player sprints to first server, who throws a ball that must be headed back from a standing or jumping position. The player then sprints to second server. This alternating continues for one minute. A passive defender can be placed to put pressure on the player working in the middle. Each player rotates as a worker and a server. Another variation using same setup and one ball: the player in the middle must flick the ball in the air to the opposite server. This focuses on redirecting the ball and defensive heading. Also, the serves can be 30 yards apart with five balls each; the player in the middle attacks a serve and must clear it high, far, and wide of the server.

Small Group Head-to-score game: 2 v 2; 10-by-15-yard grid with balls behind both end lines. Two players attack one end while defending the other end line. A team scores by scoring off a header and the shot needs to be from head height down. The shot can be saved by using any part of the body but the defenders must stay on the end line. Once the ball is saved, or the other team scores, the defending team immediately attacks the other end line and tries to score. The ball can be served from the hands, head to head, a volley, etc. Each goal is worth a point and more points can be rewarded for diving headers. Games are one minute long. Focus on heading from a standing position and heading out of the air, also proper snap through the ball and driving the ball down towards the ground.

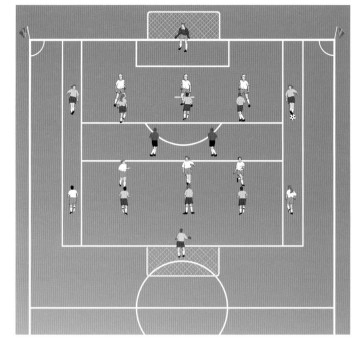

heading, large group

Large Group 3 v 3 + 3 v 3 + 2 neutrals + 4 wingers. Use a grid slightly larger than two penalty boxes. Each half of the field has three attackers and three defenders. The two neutral players in the center play both ways, and try to score goals as well.

RECEIVING

Receiving is the ability to bring a moving ball under control using various surfaces of the foot and body. The modern game of soccer requires the female player to be able to receive balls under pressure and on the run. The higher the level of competition, the faster the players are; so, it's not uncommon for a player to be challenged by two, or even more, opponents when receiving a ball. Because pressure is almost automatic in the modern game, players need to practice controlling balls under pressure.

Principles of Receiving

Approach   The controlling surface should be selected as early as possible and the player should be watching the flight path of the ball as it arrives to adjust positioning of body if needed. The part of the body that will come in contact with the ball is turning towards the ball.

Surface   The moment the ball makes contact, that part of the body being used should "give" with the ball and cushion the ball's impact.

Moving   The player's concentration should be divided between the ball and the opponent; therefore, when receiving the ball, the first touch should be used to maintain possession.

◼ Common Faults

- Player's muscles are tense at contact with ball; uncushioned, the ball ricochets away.
- Ball is allowed to bounce; giving opponent time to close down space and possibly dispossess intended receiver.
- Eyes do not meet ball as contact is made; player makes a poor first touch.
- Controlling surface is not positioned·in line with ball.
- Contact is made below midline of ball, forcing ball up into air.
- Incorrect surface area is used to receive ball.
- Ankle is not locked; ball bounces off foot unpredictably. (Foot must "give" at contact with ball, but keep ankle locked.)
- Arms hang loosely at sides; permits player to be knocked off balance

Receiving Techniques

Ground Control and Turning

Inside-the-Foot   This is the most commonly used surface to control a rolling ball along the ground. As the ball is approaching, the player should move towards the ball. This often has to be done at speed. When the controlling foot makes contact with the ball, the foot withdraws to take pace off the ball, while the body pivots on the non-kicking foot. The ball will roll across the front of the body as the player turns with the ball. This should be a fluid motion, allowing the player to continue in the opposite direction immediately out of the receiving technique. For several reasons, players should practice taking a "quick look" over their shoulder while they are sprinting, or "checking" towards a ball being played to their feet. First, this brief picture will tell a player if she can turn, and in what direction, because of pressure. Also, it will let a player know what her options are before even receiving the ball, i.e., she will receive the ball and now connect with the wide midfielder, or she will receive the ball and dribble at speed into the open space behind her.

The modern player needs to be able to improvise even in the middle of receiving a ball. For example, as a player is receiving a pass an unexpected opponent suddenly applies pressure from the side to which the player was going to run. Instead of continuing the motion forward, the player allows the receiving foot to bring the ball underneath the non-kicking leg, and then redirects the ball behind the leg, away from the pressure. The player pivots on the non-kicking foot to the outside and continues the movement forward with the ball.

Outside-the-Foot   Receiving with the outside of the foot is deemed safer simply because of the body positioning. The player can arrive square or sideways on the ball. Allowing more of her body to shield the ball from the opponent vs. using the

outside-of-foot receive

inside of the foot. As the ball arrives, the foot should be extended forward and inward. When contact is made the foot guides the ball as the body pivots on the non-kicking foot and turns in one fluid motion. Again, the player should always try and take a look at the space behind.

Aerial Control and Turning

Inside-the-Foot When attempting to control a ball of medium height and on a flight path that the body cannot get directly behind, a player should use the inside of the foot. The hardest part is moving the controlling service into its line of flight because these situations usually happen very quickly. When the ball is suddenly driven to a player, or accidentally redirected, the player must simply react— rather than have time to anticipate.

The receiving leg should be lifted and turned out from the hip, forward of the player, so that when contact is made it can be withdrawn. The point of contact with the inside of the foot should be through the midline of the ball. By continuing this motion downward and pivoting on the non-kicking foot in the direction of the ball, the player can turn and be in position to move the ball in the opposite direction.

Instep The player should move into and beneath the line of flight of the ball. The controlling leg is raised from the hip with the knee slightly bent and the toe pointing away. Contact with the ball should be made about knee height and the controlling leg should descend at a declining speed.

Once the ball has reached the ground, the player can push the ball to either side using the inside or outside of either foot or pull the ball with the sole of the receiving foot in the opposite direction.

inside-the-foot receive, air

instep receive, air

Chest The plane of the chest is dependent upon the arc of the ball being received. For example, if the ball is driven hard and straight, the player should move into the line of the flight, allowing the chest to arc back and pull away as contact is made, cushioning the ball. If the ball is dropping from a high arc a wide stance should be taken, allowing the player to get her chest underneath the ball as it drops. As the ball makes contact, the player should bend forward at the hips and lean back to position the chest to receive the ball. The arms should be extended at the sides for balance and also to hold off pressure from an opponent. When redirecting a ball with the chest, the player needs to slightly drop the shoulder closest to the direction she wants the ball to go to. As this is done the upper body pivots at the waist in the direction of the dropped shoulder, allowing the chest to redirect the ball to the space next to the player. The player continues the motion by stepping out with the foot closest to the ball and now moving on with the ball at her feet.

Thigh The player must be positioned directly behind and underneath the ball. The positioning of the thigh depends on the flight of the ball; the thigh is in a horizontal position when the ball is dropping from a high arc to just slightly bent when the flight of the ball is relatively low. As contact is made with the upper thigh, the leg gives with the ball and the foot of the contact leg drops back to the ground. The non-controlling leg should always be slightly bent to provide balance as the player cushions the ball. The ball should continue down to the ground directly in front of the player and not pop back up into the air. Even the slightest elevation of a ball off the thigh will give the opponent time to close down space and possibly dispossess the player.

When turning with a ball off the thigh, a player cannot manipulate the ball as much as her body position. As the receiving leg is withdrawing to the ground, the player can pivot off the non-kicking foot and turn her body so she is facing the opposite direction and the ball is still in front of her.

When players are young, it's good to practice these techniques from a standing position, in order to reinforce the basics. However, players even at a young age need to practice as they would actually play in a game. Sessions need to train techniques "on the move," and pressure—lack of space, time, number of opponents, difficult balls served to receiver—needs to be incorporated. As a player becomes more efficient in gaining control, her environment should become more challenging to reinforce gamelike conditions.

Practice

Receiving Ground/Aerial Balls under Pressure

Warm-Up Groups of three. Players pass to each other in area (top of 18-yard box to midfield line). One ball per group and each player will control a pass from one partner and try to turn in the direction of the other partner who is jogging in the area. Then she will pass a ball to the other partner who will do the same. Focus on change of pace when approaching a ball, controlling in a direction both on the ground and in the air, taking a look to find the partner before receiving the ball.

Individual Same group of three, one server, one defender, and one attacker. Play in a 20-by-30-yard area, and a goal or end line can be used. Server delivers aerial and ground balls in to attacker, who must control and turn using the appropriate parts of her body. The defender can start out passive, but should be 100% involved by the end of the practice. Now the attacker must decide what direction the pressure will come from. Focus on taking a look at the opponent during the approach to the ball, using the arms for balance and as guides to feel for pressure.

1

2

3

4

chest trap, charging

receiving, small group

Small Group Play 3 v 2 + 3 v 2 + 2 goalkeepers to big goals. Two half-field grids. Three players possess and try to pass to two target players who are being defended by three players. The target players must control passes delivered from the opposite grid and cannot pass the ball back in the beginning of the practice. This forces the player to control and turn under pressure, using various serves but also implementing tactical decision-making with teammates. Eventually, targets can combine with midfielders and the game becomes continuous. Focus on technique of controlling and turning in the direction that allows possession.

Large Group Play 8 v 8 to 11 v 11, large goals. Team must connect ten passes together before going to the goal, but at least one of those passes has to be in the air. Focus on control and turning in different areas of the field.

TACKLING

Tackling is the ability to regain possession by taking the ball directly away from an opponent. The tactical element to tackling is anticipating the dribbling action of the opponent and picking the precise time to make a proper tackle. There are several different types of tackle, and part of tackling success is due to choosing the proper tackle needed in a given situation.

Because tackling is very confrontational and physical contact is almost always made, many young girls have trouble finding the will or mindset to tackle. The cause could be a fear of becoming injured, or of not knowing how to do it correctly, or simply not wanting to be stereotyped as being a "brute." It is important that young women learn the proper techniques at an early age, because good tackling is a must at the higher levels of competition. It is also a safety issue for both players involved in the tackle. If at all possible, the player should tackle with the back foot, as this allows both power and balance when tackling.

Principles of Tackling

Approach The player must be at the proper distance when making the tackle, not too far away from the opponent and not too close to her before making the tackle.

Timing Attempt the tackle at the right time; i.e., not too early and not too late. This can be dictated by the player's positioning on the field; such as, if an opponent has possession inside your 18-yard box there is no room for delay. The tackle needs to happen quickly.

Mentality The player needs to be confident and motivated when making the tackle, focusing only on winning the ball.

block tackle

Strength   The player needs to be strong and powerful in the legs and upper body because both areas are used often during tackles (shoulder tackle, block tackle). Also, she needs to be agile and flexible enough while attempting tackles from the ground (slide tackle). In all types of tackle, the muscles and joints should be tightened as contact is made with the ball and the opponent.

Common Faults
- Diving in too soon; not anticipating the dribble
- Delaying tackle too long
- Not aggressive/focused enough on winning ball; opponent maintains possession
- Choosing wrong style of tackle for positioning of opponent; foul/injury can occur
- Using wrong foot

Tackling Techniques

Block Tackle   Both players are in facing positions and are moving directly towards each other. The defending player uses her whole body on the tackle and blocks the ball by applying pressure with the inside of the foot. Often, players will try to kick the ball instead of block it, resulting in less power being used. When block tackling, full body weight is used instead of just the leg kicking the ball.

shoulder tackle

Shoulder Tackle   Both players are running side by side towards an oncoming ball or a ball being pushed in front of them. When the ball is in close proximity, shoulder contact can legally be made as long as the elbows are not raised. When contact with the ball is imminent, the defender can gain positioning by dropping the touching shoulder and sliding the upper body in front of the opponent. This will allow her to bring her body into the path of the ball and screen her opponent.

Slide Tackle   The players are positioned alongside each other and the opponent is dribbling the ball. When the opponent is about to touch the ball again (to pass, shoot, or dribble), the defender attempts to block the ball by shifting her weight back and pushing off either leg to swing the opposite leg in the path of the opponent while sliding on the ground. The inside or the outside of the foot can be used; it depends on the order of the steps taken.

1

2

3

4

slide tackle

5

poke tackle

Poke Tackle   As in the shoulder tackle, both players are positioned side by side. As the opponent is dribbling down the field, the defender applies pressure to the attacker by using her shoulder and, with the outside of the foot nearest the opponent, she kicks the ball away. This tackle is often used while defending along the sideline. It is not used to regain possession, but merely to knock the ball out of bounds.

2

Systems of Play

There are various types of tactical formation, called systems, to consider for use; such as:
1) 4-3-3; 2) 3-4-3; 3) 4-4-2; 4) 3-5-2; 5) 4-5-1.

Regardless of the system being played, all are influenced by numerous factors: the technical and tactical strengths and weaknesses of your players; strengths and weaknesses of your opponent; the type of system your opponent is playing; the weather; the playing surface; game situations (up a goal, down a goal); an injury sustained by a player in the middle of the game; the day and time of game (first game of a double-header weekend); a home vs. away game; and the physical condition of a team.

In today's modern game of soccer, a coach must have an understanding of various tactical systems in order to properly prepare her or his team. The days of the strict man-to-man system with two marking backs is long gone. Players and coaches must be more flexible in their tactical approach to the game. Still, some coaches prefer one particular system and, regardless of the type of player they have available, will constantly use that favored system. Another coach might consistently change the team's system on a yearly basis, or a game-by-game basis. There is no right or wrong to this — each system has its strengths and its weaknesses. What coaches need to become familiar with is

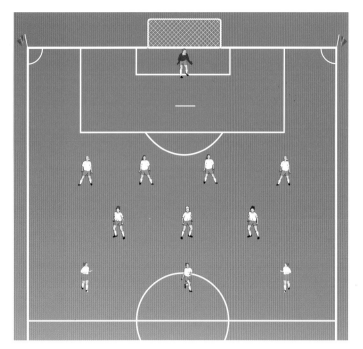

4-3-3

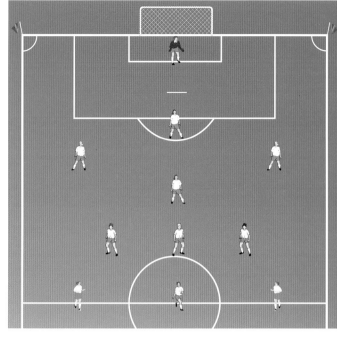

4-3-3 sweep

how to attack and defend against each particular system of play.

Some basics to remember when playing within any system are:

- Players should be evenly spaced over the entire field.
- Each player should have specific responsibilities.
- Players must be able to switch from defense to offense very quickly.
- If needed, players can switch positions and adjust tactically, creating variations within a system.
- It's the players that win games, not the system.

4-3-3 System

4 defenders, 3 midfielders, 3 forwards

Advantages
- Both wing players are already in place, providing width and a very balanced attack. This allows

teams to change the point of attack easily. With the addition of a center forward the three attackers are already in position every time the ball is won.

- Having three forwards allows the team to apply pressure on the ball immediately upon losing possession. It also allows a team to play very direct because there are three options up top vs. having only one or two. For this reason, it's a great system if your team happens to be down a goal and needs to create scoring opportunities in the attacking third. Also, it is effective when playing a team that lacks longer service out of the back or has a particularly weak defender, because pressure will constantly be placed on this particular player, who will more than likely turn the ball over.
- The system does not allow opponents room to change the point of attack out of the back, forcing a direct style of play. This makes it predictable for the midfield and defense to intercept balls played forward by the opposing team.
- Most teams will play with four defenders vs. a three-front system, taking one more player out of their attack.

- By utilizing three forwards, a coach can play a less fit player or a slower player up top. This is a less taxing system on the forwards. Using a two-front system, both players must be fit and somewhat speedy.
- Because a team has committed three players forward, this relays an attacking mentality both to the team playing the system and the team defending against the system. It's often a fun and exciting system to play and watch because it welcomes the attacking mentality and getting the ball into the attacking third.
- Having four defenders still provides a balanced defense that can handle three opposing attackers without having to adjust to lower numbers up front.

Disadvantages

- By using only three midfielders, a coach must be sure the players are quite mobile, able to cover a lot of ground. Problems could occur in the covering of space and the midfielder's ability to press forward in the attack because of being outnumbered in the midfield.
- Loss of flexibility up top and in the midfield by establishing definite positions with three forwards. Becomes predictable to defend if they lack mobility and constantly play back to goal.
- A very easy system for the other team to recognize; three players up top can be bypassed by one forward pass from the opponent's defense, leaving only seven field players to defend.
- Having only three midfielders creates problems in the covering of space and the ability to press forward in the attack when needed. A team can be outnumbered in the midfield constantly.

When to Use 4-3-3

- Your team needs a goal to avoid a loss; therefore immediate pressure is needed in the attacking third every time possession is lost.
- Your team is a very direct-style team with the ability to serve balls into the attacking third, and you have forwards who have the ability to receive balls and combine with one another.
- You have slower players that have difficulty defending or covering a lot of ground up top.
- You are playing against a 4-4-2 man-to-man system, allowing your forwards to manipulate the defensive shape of the opposing team and crowd or clear certain areas of the attacking third. In addition, you can easily defend against the two-front system while allowing a defender to push into the midfield when pressing forward as a team or sharing midfield defensive responsibilities.

3-4-3 System

3 defenders, 4 midfielders, 3 forwards

Advantages

- The same advantages are created in the attacking third, when using three forwards in the 3-4-3, as in the 4-3-3.

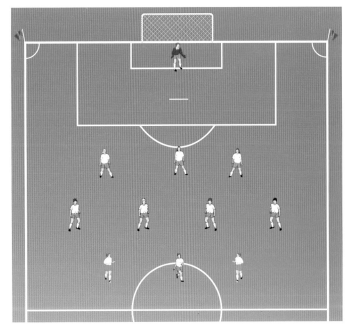

3-4-3

- Having four midfielders creates a more balanced attack, and a more unpredictable attack because now seven players can be involved in the attacking third at any given time.
- The ability to press the ball in the attacking third, once it is lost, is increased because numbers are more than likely even in the midfield third, which provides a more balanced defense.
- Increased chances of winning balls in the midfield because now an extra defender has been pushed up from the back into the midfield third.

Disadvantages

- By using only three defenders, a coach must make sure these players are quite fit and fast, with the ability to cover a lot of ground and win balls in the air. There is not as much room for error with only three defenders. The three backs could play a zone or man-to-man marking with a sweeper.
- Loss of ability to attack out of the back third because of the lack of width. Also players must become conservative with service and decisions on when to push forward because of lack of numbers.
- Loss of ability to change the point of attack out of the back; must rely on the midfield to do this.
- Become very susceptible to long driven balls and diagonal balls served over the midfield because of the spacing behind the outside midfielders. This is especially true if the team is playing man to man with a sweeper in the back because of the other team's ability to manipulate the defenders to one side and open up an outside area.
- Seven players can be bypassed by one pass from the opponent when pressure is lacking on the ball.

When to Use 3-4-3

- Your team needs a goal; therefore, immediate pressure is needed in the attacking and midfield thirds to regain possession.

- You are playing vs. a 4-4-2 system and your back three can play a man-to-man or zone coverage, depending on your use of a sweeper or not.
- Your back three are quite athletic and fast with the ability to serve long balls into the attacking third or connect with a shorter pass into the midfield.
- You have a very athletic goalkeeper who is quick off her line and has tremendous foot skills. This relieves pressure on the back three by allowing them to use the goalkeeper as an outlet when balls are won. In addition, the goalie can win balls served behind the defensive line instead of the defenders' having to chase down every ball.

4-4-2 System

4 defenders, 4 midfielders, 2 forwards

Advantages

- The midfield is strengthened by one more player and the entire system is more defensively oriented than a three-front system.
- Defenders have opportunities to join the attack with less defensive responsibilities because of increased numbers in the back and midfield.
- The ability to change the point of attack out of the back and in the midfield, making the team unpredictable to defend and successfully press.
- Flanks are very active, attacking opportunities by overlapping outside defenders, penetrating on the dribble by outside midfielders, or penetrating runs by two target players or a central midfielder.
- Much more space in the attacking third allows for increased mobility out of the two target players, and midfielders have room to push forward.
- Two target players can manipulate the opposing team's defense by compacting them centrally by serving as double targets in front of the opponent's goal.

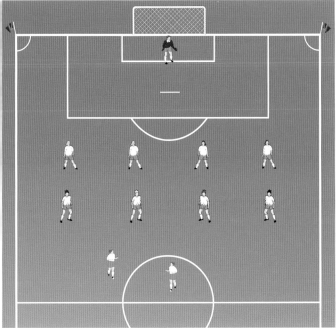

4-4-2

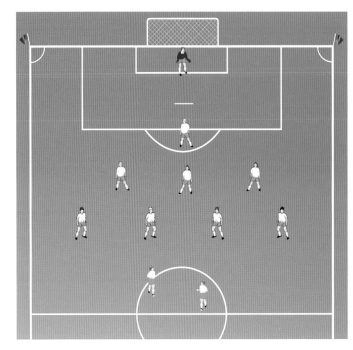

4-4-2 sweep

- There are consistently eight field players behind the ball denying penetration.
- Very easy system for players to keep their shape.

Disadvantages

- The two outside defensive positions are not constantly covered, allowing for quick counter-attacks from the opponents outside defenders. This requires much more defensive responsibilities for the outside midfielders and often they can be faced with a 2 v 1 situation.
- Opponents have more space to change the point of attack out of their defensive third and more time to serve balls over the midfield into your defensive third.
- You have a numbers-down situation in the midfield, when the opposing team commits an extra player into the midfield on attack.
- Target players can be pressed too far forward and find themselves isolated from teammates.

When to Use 4-4-2

- Your team is up a goal and wants to protect the lead.
- Your team has very good tactical skills with players who have the physical ability to switch from midfield and forward positions.
- You are playing against a three-front system.
- You have fast and skillful forwards.
- You have slower central defenders who cannot cover a lot of ground and like to stay central.
- Your goalkeeper is lacking in experience or talent, so your main priority is to keep numbers in front of the ball and not allow penetration on the flanks or shots on goal.
- Your team has a good understanding of zonal defending, allowing players to get involved in the attack often.

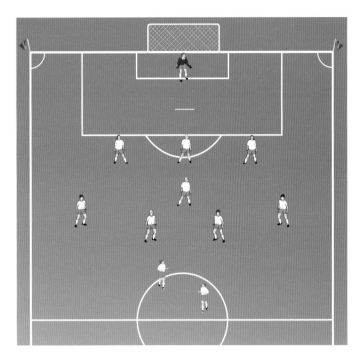

3-5-2

3-5-2 System

Advantages

- A very confusing system for the opposing team to break down in the midfield.
- Immediate pressure is placed on the ball when the opposing team tries to play through the midfield.
- Ability to cover a lot of space in the midfield and press players forward into the attack.
- Transition from defense to attack is quicker because of numbers in the midfield.
- Constant and close support to the two forwards from the three central players.
- Ability to shunt opponent centrally into a crowded and heavily defended area by having two wide forwards.
- The system is very flexible and allows various players to attack and defend at different times.

Disadvantages

- A lot of defensive responsibility is put on your outside midfielders because of the large space behind the outside backs.
- Lack of pressure on the ball in attacking third can result in one pass that will bypass five midfielders and leave three defenders isolated.
- Roles in the midfield can be confusing as to marking responsibilities; communication is a must.
- Lack of space in the midfield can crowd players and stifle creativity once the ball is won.
- Having only three defenders requires them to penetrate by passing and not on the dribble or run.

When to Use 3-5-2

- Your team has a smart, talented free player in the back with two fast and strong marking backs.
- You have a talented but slow central player who you want to hide in the midfield.
- You are playing against a 4-4-2 system.
- Your opponent has a very talented central player that needs to be marked at all times, and sometimes double-teamed.
- You have very fit and fast flank players who have the ability to cover a lot of ground.
- You have a central player that is fit and fast with the ability to make diagonal runs forward and join the attack constantly.
- Your opponent has a very indirect style and is not effective in serving long direct passes, so they must play through the midfield.
- Your central midfielders have a solid understanding of the system arrangement, e.g., two defensive midfielders and one attacking midfielder, or one attacking midfielder, one organizer, and one defensive midfielder.

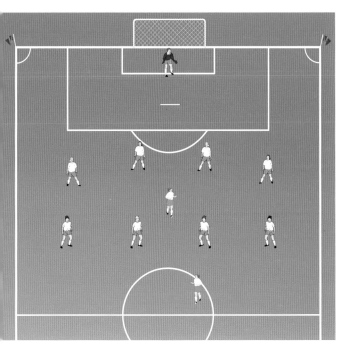

4-5-1

4-5-1 System

4 defenders, 5 midfielders, 1 forward

Advantages

- A defense-oriented system that is very hard to penetrate with nine players behind the ball.
- Easy for a less talented team to protect their goal and keep a game close.
- Flanks are covered from behind with four defenders, allowing flank players and a central midfielder to push into the attacking third consistently.
- Transition out of the back and in the midfield is quick because of numbers committed to these areas.
- Great system for low pressure to generate a quick counter because the opposing team has committed too many players forward.

Disadvantages

- Offensive opportunities are consistently generated through the midfield, making a team predictable to defend.
- Opponent can push players into the attack because of lack of pressure in their defensive third and can press because of only having to mark one forward.
- Easy to shut down only one target player, who can get frustrated and tire easily; also must be able to hold the ball.
- Space in the defensive and midfield third is crowded, making it difficult to play a shorter style if you don't have talented playmakers.
- The basic demand of players being spread evenly over the field is not met.
- Very difficult for one forward to make the opposing team predictable when attacking out of their defensive third.

When to Use 4-5-1

- Your team is a goal up and needs to protect a lead against a very strong and talented team.
- You have a strong athletic forward who has the ability to hold onto balls and combine with midfielders.
- Your team is very good at zonal defending, communicates well, and has strong organizers in the middle of the field.
- Your opponent is playing a 3-5-3 or a 3-5-2 and is high pressing.
- Your main objective is not to score but to prevent scoring from your opponent.

Shaping the Team

It is important that players have a good under-standing of their roles on the field, specifically with regard to the three "thirds of the field."

The best way for a coach to foster this under-standing is by providing players with a solid foundation on the principles of play.

Principals of Play

BALL POSSESSION

ATTACKING	TRANSITION	DEFENDING
penetration (depth)		immediate chase / pressure
width		delay
support		cover / depth
mobility		concentration
improvisation		balance

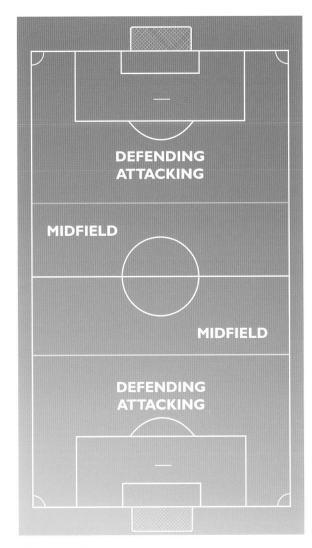

thirds of field

Midfield Third

Actually, the midfield third can itself be divided into two halves: a defending half (closer to your goal) and an attacking half (closer to the attacking third). When your team has possession of the ball in the defending half of the midfield third, there should be some concern for safety and risk. In the attacking half, there is more room for risk than safety. This will have to do with the position of the ball and how far away it is from your own goal. In addition, this can be flexible, based on the strength of your midfield (weaker central player vs. best player on the team).

When possession is won in midfield, the first priority is to penetrate as soon as possible. If not, the team must maintain possession until they get the chance to go forward. When possession is lost, the first priority is to delay penetration through pressure. This will allow teammates to get goal-side.

Attacking Third

In the attacking third of the field, you should encourage your players to take risks. High risks = high rewards = goals = winning games.

In this third of the field, there will be many bodies and limited time and space to operate, unless the attacking team is entering their zone through counterattacking.

Because of the tightness in this third, players should be encouraged to take players on 1 v 1 and must be able to break teams down through combination play (1-2's, even 1-3's—three-man combination). Coaches should foster this attitude by encouraging players to take on the forwards often during training, playing 1 v 2 or 2 v 3. This organization is true to the real game environment because forwards consistently have to beat more than one defender to get to the goal.

Defending Third

When a team has possession of the ball in their own defensive third, the first priority is safety. Passing options in this third, while in possession and passing, should be limited to those with very low risk. When defending in this third, the first priority is, of course, to not give up a goal. However, some risk may be taken in order to win the ball and stop goal-scoring chances. The acceptable risks depend on individual and team considerations, and proper defensive shape.

On the defending side, the striker will be the first line of defense. A striker has to make play predictable through her organization. Considerations here are the starting positions and the speed and angle of the approach to the opposition. Also, the number of forwards in the formation will determine what type of defending the forwards will try to achieve: two target players vs. three forwards.

SHADOW PLAY

One of the problems all coaches face is a short preseason period. This problem can be compounded by changing rosters, injuries, poor fitness, and the attrition factor. During preseason, a coach will try to provide any or all new players with a team understanding of attacking and defending. In addition to teaching thirds of field, a method of training that helps to facilitate the attacking side of ball handling is shadow-play.

Shadow play is a way of training through set play patterns as well as free play, without opposition—no physical opponent to play against. In shadow play, however, there is *mental* opposition that, to utilize properly, calls for a high degree of soccer imagination.

Shadow-Play Practice

Start shadow-play exercise by playing 11 v 1 on a full field, the one being the opposing goalkeeper. The coach stands near the top of the 18-yard box with a supply of soccer balls. The team of eleven should start in a defensive posture in its own half of the field. A ball is served to the goalkeeper. As the ball is traveling, the team moves into proper wide-and-high positions, creating a good team

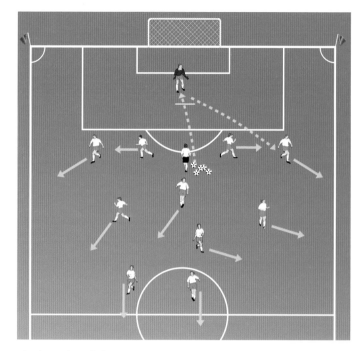

shadow play, defensive

shape from which to attack. This shape should help create time and space for the team. The coach or the goalkeeper can choose to whom and how to distribute the ball.

At the beginning, the team should play the ball down the field, as well as move forward with the play. The object is to finish with a shot on goal. Once that has been made, the coach can have the team start from that end and return to the original end. During the first few shadow play runs, the coach should not expect too much from the team.

Coaching Challenges

The primary challenge is to get the players to "play the game" as realistically as possible (valid supporting angles and distances, quality and decisionmaking of the pass), playing against an opponent who is not really there. In this regard, shadow play requires a lot of imagination from the players, and patience from the coach. Once the players do get the idea behind shadow play, some of the challenges a coach may encounter are:

- Inappropriate spacing of the players in relation to the ball, and of the team's movement in relation to the ball
- Too many short passes in the same field area
- Playing in the same direction for too long
- Unrealistic-type passes
- Playing too slow
- Players not using their imaginations
- Players forgetting the offside rule

Developing Play

To focus on fast positioning and urgency, change the starting position of the shadow-playing team: for example, start at midfield and play in the attacking half of the field.

The next step in developing shadow play is for the coach to introduce a pattern of play for the team to follow. These patterns are to help get the team "on the same page." However, coaches must remember that this is soccer, not American football where set play-book patterns are the norm.

The third step is to place more pressure on the eleven players. This can be accomplished by implementing some simple restrictions, such as: 1) set a touch limitation for the team; 2) the ball is not allowed to stop rolling; 3) play 11 v 4.

In the 11 v 4 practice, the four are made up of a goalkeeper, a defender, a midfielder, and a forward. If the ball is touched by one of the eleven defending players, play stops, then starts over.

Setting these types of restriction helps to increase the speed of movement and the speed at which the players take up supporting angles and distances.

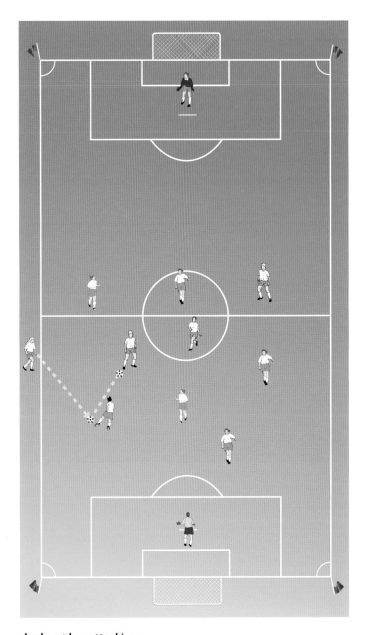

shadow play, attacking

11 v 11 shadow play

The final step is to play 11 v 11. Each team starts in its own half of the field with both goal-keepers in possession of a ball. Simultaneously, both goalkeepers begin play. Each team then shadow plays up the field. The process of having the teams play at the same time will create a natural sense of opposition because of the numbers of players actually on the field, and the opening and closing of spaces. Both teams should finish with shots on goal. The teams then turn around and shadow-play back.

Man-to-Man vs. Zonal Defense

When playing man-to-man marking, the psychological and physical attributes of the players and of the opponents have to be taken into consideration. The defending player will be required to cover her opponent all over the field, so she must be psychologically strong. In actuality, this tactic creates ten 1 v 1 situations all over the field.

To be successful with the man-to-man system, the team needs to have a very good sweeper who will establish rhythm, cover, and good decision-making as to when to attack.

Weaknesses of Man-to-Man System

- System is not physically economical for players.
- Psychologically, players can become preoccupied with marking, and not attack.
- Defenders can be "dragged" into bad positions, which can destroy good team shape.
- Causes a lack of imagination and flexibility.
- Impedes the development of a player into a "complete" soccer player.

Zonal Defending

The zone defense has been a part of world soccer for a long time, but the concept burst onto the United States scene after the 1994 Men's World Cup. Three out of four teams played zone, including Brazil, who won the championship! Having had the opportunity, and privilege, of coaching both men and women, I have found some type of zone play to be very effective and efficient in women's soccer. This is mainly due to the fact that certain physical attributes of women are limited compared to men. Women cannot strike a ball as far as men and do not run as fast as men. With these factors taken into account, the zone concept is, for women's soccer, very appealing. The first thing that a coach must decide is how high his/her team is going to defend up the field (the restraining line). Then a solid team understanding of the principle of playing under pressure and how it applies to zonal defending must be developed.

There are three different starting positions where the team can start to apply pressure: 1) top of the penalty box—full pressure; 2) 30 yards out from the other team's goal—middle pressure; 3) from the midfield line—low pressure.

A coach decides where the team will establish the restraining line based on these considerations:

- The physical and psychological characteristics of the teams (strikers). For example, if the strikers are fast, they may be ideal for counterattacking. So the restraining line should be deep; i.e., midfield. If the strikers are not fast, but have different qualities, for example, strong heading of the ball, their restraining line should be higher.
- The physical condition of the players. Will the fitness of your team allow you to have a high restraining line?
- How strong is the other team? If the other team is weaker, the pressure should be high. If the other team is equal, then the pressure should be established at the attacking third of the field. If the other team is stronger, the pressure (high) should be at the halfway line.
- The particular situations of the game: the team is a goal up or down, it's a home game or away, various weather conditions.

Key Elements of the Zone Defense

- Principles of defending must be understood: delay of the opposition's penetration, cover, balance, concentration, control, and restraint.
- The team must be clear about the position of the restraining line for high pressure, middle pressure, and low pressure.
- Players generally must cover all the dangerous areas of the field.
- Inside vs. outside; defending team must be "on the same page" on where to push the opponent.

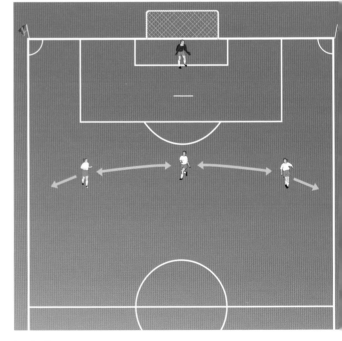

back three

- Compact space vertically (short) and horizontally (tight) to cut off passing lanes and control the opposition by controlling the spaces.
- Promote an understanding and tactical awareness of the dangerous runs; inside to outside is less dangerous than outside to inside. Square runs are more dangerous vs. diagonal runs behind a defense.
- Midfielders must recognize when to pass players on, and when to track players.
- Front players must do their parts to make play predictable through their proper angle of approach toward defenders.
- The team must shift with the ball during the time of flight.
- Defending players must know where teammates are in relation to their own position.
- The team must be in set shape to attack when they regain possession.
- Goalkeeper must become more vertical.

PRACTICES

The practices that follow provide you with ways to put in a back three, a back four, or even a back five. Simply modify them to fit the team's needs. However, the coach must understand that she/he must instill the principles of play into the players or zonal play will not work.

1 v 1

In a 20-by-10 grid, player A passes the ball to player B. Player B begins dribbling with the intention of beating player A and carrying the ball over the end line. Player A follows her pass in order to place pressure on player B. If player A dispossesses player B, roles are reversed.

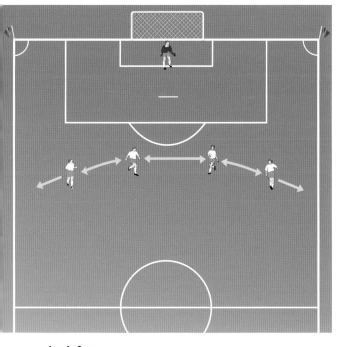

back four

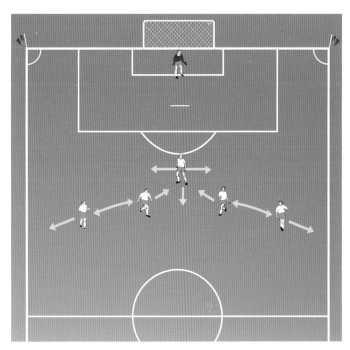

back five

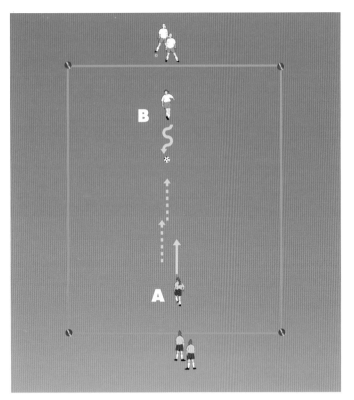

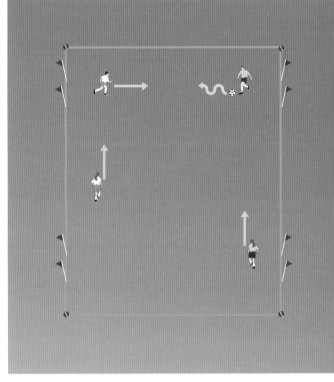

1 v 1

2 v 2

Key Coaching Points (defender)

- Speed of approach, to stop penetration
- Proper angle of approach
- When to slow down; e.g., as attacking player is about to touch ball
- Taking proper sideways-on stance
- Making play predictable through the angle of approach
- Importance of not allowing attacking player to cut back on the dribble

2 v 2

In a 30-by-20 grid, using 4 goals, each defending duo is responsible for their two goals. Any of the attacking players can score a goal by playing or dribbling through the cone goals. Third players can be placed in a forward position; i.e., target player. The purpose of using cone goals is to help develop the concept of space marking and the principles of pressure, cover, and communication.

Key Coaching Points

- Nearest player applies pressure on ball.
- Second defender provides cover based on positions of other attacking players and the goals.
- Covering player should position herself to inside of ball and goal.
- The covering player must also cover the space *behind* pressuring player, and be deep enough to see the ball and other attacking player without turning.
- It's important to communicate.
- Defenders should not chase ball, but pass players on.
- Defenders must not cross over in front of each other.
- Players need to coordinate their moves; stepping up or dropping off at the same time.

6 v 6

Play is on half-field. The players must be coached to understand that the starting position of zonal marking is predicated on where the ball is, the position of the opponent, and the goal. The marking players need to be goal-side and ball-side. The reasoning is, can the defender step up and intercept the pass? If not, can she intercept the ball off the attacking player's first touch? A player's goal- and ball-side positioning allows that opportunity. However, when the ball is deep on the field, the marking can even be in front of the attacker.

Key Coaching Points

- Back four's primary marking responsibility is space, not players. (You can run, but you cannot hide!)
- Players in back four must communicate.
- Combine pressure, cover, and balance.
- A player's position is off the inside shoulder of each player, to allow for distance and angle for recovery run.
- Players step up with forwards who come off the two central backs, so as not to allow them to turn and face the back four. The other three players should pitch in.
- Players must understand that runs from inside to out are less dangerous than runs from outside to in.
- Space can be stolen when ball is played square or backwards. (Move while the ball is moving!)

Types of Defending Line

Defending on the diagonal One of the outside backs pressures the ball, while the other three support off the inside shoulder to cover their teammates and spaces. This arrangement makes it very difficult to recover if/when the ball is switched. Also it's very hard to set the offsides trap from this alignment.

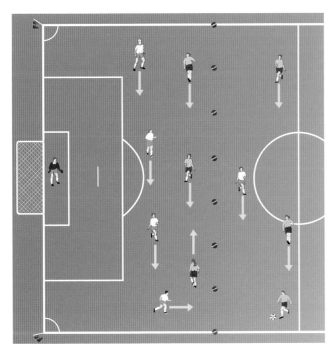

6 v 6

defending on diagonal

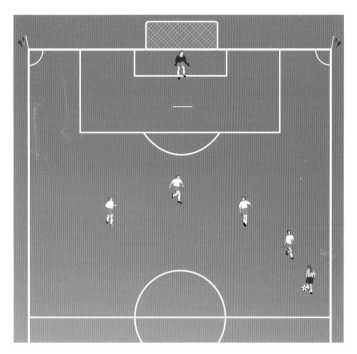

three-line defending

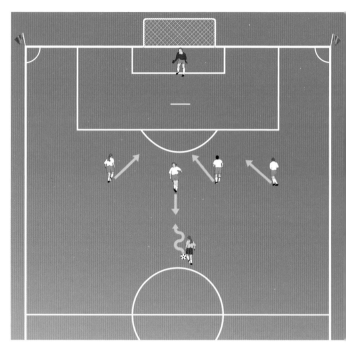

triangle defense (before)

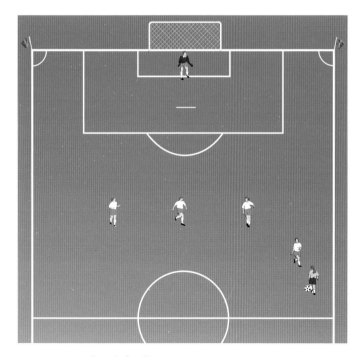

two-line defending

Three-line defending   The ball can be pressed by the outside back and two covering players, while the balancing player steps up even with the first covering player. The starting position of the balancing player allows her to be in a realistic position to intercept a long switched pass, or at least put pressure on the ball.

Two-line defending   Again, the outside back presses the ball, but the covering player and two others stay on the same defensive line. This is the easiest alignment to set the offside trap. It also requires the goalkeeper to act more as a sweeper. Remember, the goalkeeper must be coached in all of these exercises, whether you are playing a back three, four, or five.

Triangle defense   When dealing with attacks down the middle, the defensive unit will form a triangle shape, with the apex of the triangle putting pressure on the ball. The other central defender and the two outside backs provide cover on a single line.

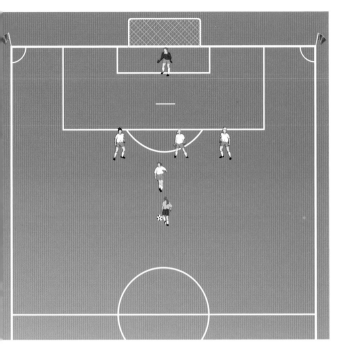

triangle defense (after)

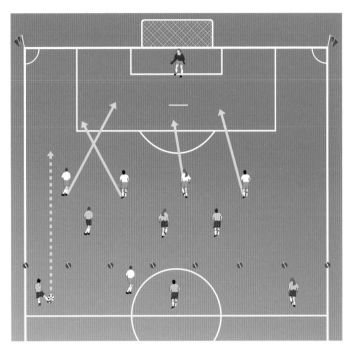

covering example 1

If the game demands that the two central backs must defend in the last 20 yards, they then shift from a zonal marking to a man-to-man marking situation, picking up the last attacker entering the area. The coach must also get the message across that runs from inside to out are less dangerous than runs from outside to in. The outside-to-in run attacks the space directly behind the defense; the inside-to-out run does not. It is important for defenders to track runners who are running from outside to in.

The covering positions of the support players are critical to making proper recovery runs when needed. Shown here are some examples:

In example 1, each player is positioned off the inside shoulder of the player she is covering. The right fullback recovers to the inside, using the near post as a visual cue. The nearest central defender sprints out to put pressure on the ball. The other central defender recovers to the center of the goal, using the penalty spot as a visual cue, and the left fullback recovers to the center of the goal.

In example 2, the principles are the same.

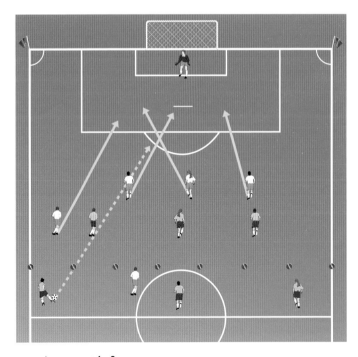

covering example 2

4 v 1

There are times when an attacking player will run crossfield, in front of the back four. To train the back four to handle this problem, here's a good exercise.

Key Coaching Points

- In play, defending back four should be alert to a cross-run attack.
- First defender pressures the ball and stays with ball carrier until called off.
- Covering players position themselves off inside shoulder for proper cover and balance.
- When in position, covering player calls off pressing player. (Don't get caught in the switch!)
- Attacking players come from both sides of the field.

6 v 4

Key Coaching Points

- Move while the ball is moving.
- Mark space, not attacker, but only when the attackers come into the zone.
- Seal off certain space.
- Step up when ball is played back; pressing out is unpredictable and can surprise opposing team, resulting in turnovers.

Midfield

When putting in the midfield, the principles are the same, but now the coach must decide on the shape of the midfield. There are many ways for a coach to organize the midfield, based on the players available. Some possibilities are: four across, attacking or defensive midfield, and box or diamond formations.

4 v 1

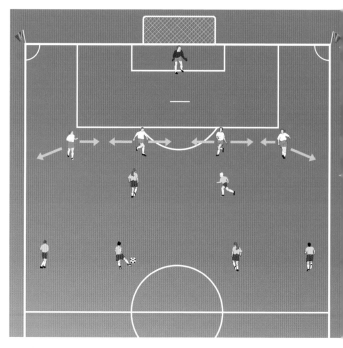

6 v 4

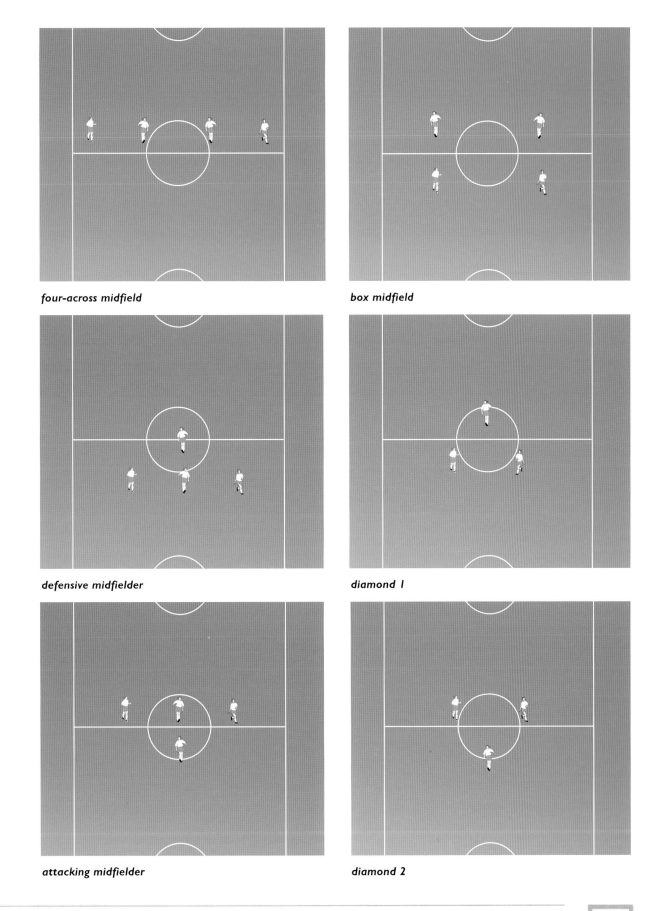

four-across midfield

box midfield

defensive midfielder

diamond 1

attacking midfielder

diamond 2

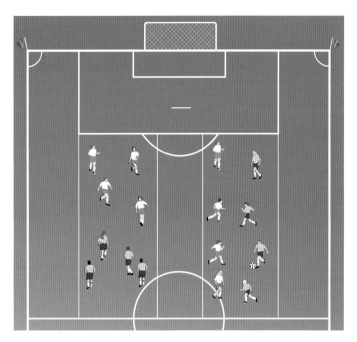

4 v 4

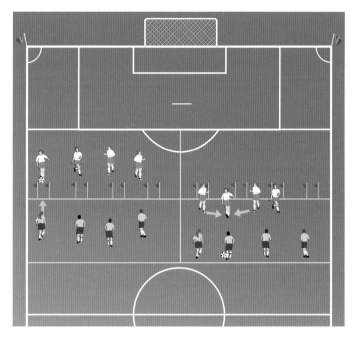

four-gate defense

Exercises

Start off with a type of 2 v 2 exercise to instill the principles of pressure and cover. The next stage is 4 v 4 on a horizontal field, then on a vertical field. This allows the players to work in groups of two. In 4 v 4 practice, the team in possession scores goals by carrying the ball over the line.

Four-gate defense   For the next set of exercises, four players defend four gates. The attacking team can advance only by dribbling through one of the four gates. Defending behind the gates represents low pressure. Defending in front of the gates represents high pressure.

First, a coach can have players practice pushing the team inside or outside. The angle of approach of the nearest defender should be straight to the ball, not bent. This will stop vertical passing options. The speed of approach, the covering position, and the balancing position should also be dealt with in this practice.

8 v 8   The next step is to put the back and midfield lines together. In this practice exercise, you play 8 v 8 with three gates at midfield. The coach needs to work on the cohesion of the two

lines and getting players to move while the ball is moving (time of flight), and also work on pushing inside or outside and double teaming.

The team in possession must play through one of the three gates before they can enter the other half of the field to then attack the goal. This can be accomplished by passing the ball through, dribbling through, and even throw-ins. When the attacking team breaks through, the defending team must quickly get goal-side and ball-side of the attacking team and organize themselves.

Key Coaching Points

- Nearest defending player pressures the ball.
- Covering players mark goal-side and ball-side.
- Balancing players must push over and up to compact space both vertically and horizontally.
- Two lines work together to cut off passing lanes and marking players around the ball.
- Stress communication.

The final step now is getting your strikers organized on how and where they are going to defend. Practices should incorporate the concepts of pressure and cover.

8 v 8

striker defense 1

striker/forwards mark outside

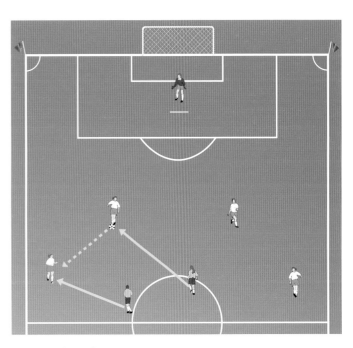

striker defense 2

Two striker/forwards can mark to cut passes to the outside backs and to force the two central defenders to play with the ball at their feet. In many cases the outside backs are better passers of the ball than the two central defenders are. By cutting out this outlet, it will force the two central defenders to play and start the attack.

11 v 11 zone

Man-to-Man vs. Zonal Defense

11 v 11 Zone

In the 11 v 11 game, the field is divided into three vertical and three horizontal channels. The defending players cannot be more than two zones away from the ball. This will help work with the team's shape vertically and horizontally.

Key Coaching Points

- Nearest player puts immediate pressure to the ball.
- Players around the ball must get ball-side and goal-side to cut down passing angles.
- Force the play inside.
- Balance players to squeeze the space both vertically and horizontally.
- Goalkeeper must act as a sweeper.

Disadvantages of Zonal Defending

- Zonal is not the standard defense system for most U.S. players and teams.
- System demands verbal communication and hard vertical movement defensively.
- It's difficult to man-mark an exceptional player while implementing a zonal defense.
- Backs can get caught square/flat.
- Goalkeeper may become a back-sweeper.

Advantages of Zonal Defending

- In the United States, few coaches or players have seen enough of zonal defending to know how to break it down.
- A team made up of less-proficient players can compete against superior teams—especially in the women's game.
- The system is based purely on the principles of play, enhancing the flexibility of players within the system.
- Transition is easier when the team regains possession.
- The goalkeeper is more connected to the rest of the team.

- Players seem to like it. Why? It is less taxing physically: everyone defends, everyone attacks. Women like the "teamwork"—not just one person responsible for an opposing star. *All* must shut that player down. Keeps players from finger-pointing!

Countering on Zone Defense

- One teammate is left uncommitted behind central midfielders, as shown. To counter this, one of the central defenders pushes onto the attacking player in the hole.
- Attack along the whole width of the field by quick changes of the point of attack.
- Use mobility of the strikers to clear space for players to run into from deep positions. Forwards and midfielders must be very mobile and committed to more diagonal runs off the ball to confuse and pull apart zone.

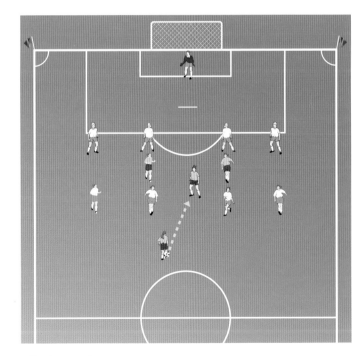

attack zone 1

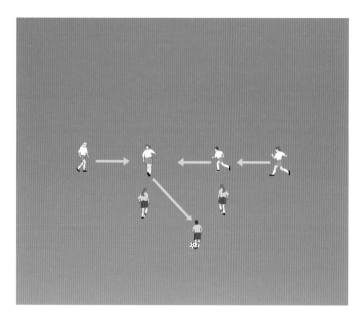

attack zone (counter) 2

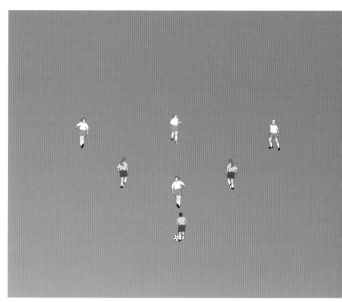

attack zone (counter) 3

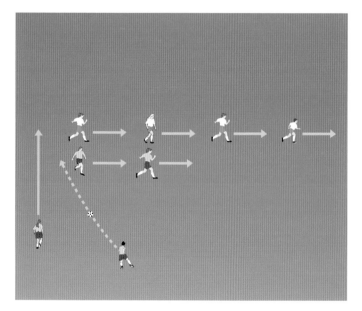

striker mobility

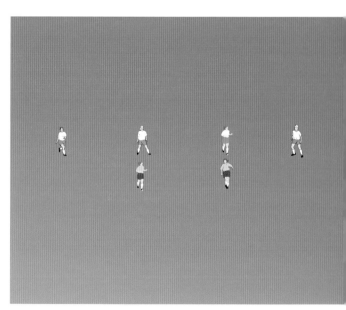

forward back-push

- Have the two forwards push against the two central defenders. This prevents the two central defenders from applying support cover inside and on the flanks.

- Long direct punts and dropkicks from the goal-keeper, as the two forwards push onto the two central defenders; again, looking for flicks and knockdowns.

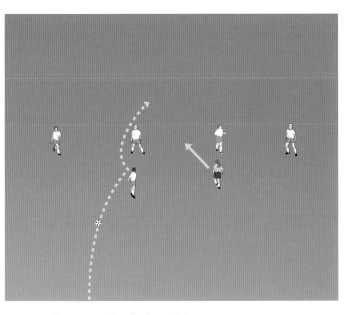

long punt/dropkick to flick

Zone–Man Mark Combination

This system combines covering specific zones while, at the same time, marking a special opponent, or simply marking the player with the ball and potential support players when they happen to enter the zone (match-up zone).

In reality, this is what happens when a team plays zone. You put pressure on the ball and stop penetration. The tighter the pressure on the ball (forcing the player's head down); the tighter the covering positions of all the other defending players.

In the women's game, you see this defense a lot. A lot of teams, for example, play 3-5-2. This system is made up of a sweeper and two man-markers; five midfielders, who play a combination of zone in the central area of the midfield and more man-to-man in the flank channels; then two strikers, who will zone-mark when the ball is central and will press to the ball when it is wide.

zone–man mark defense

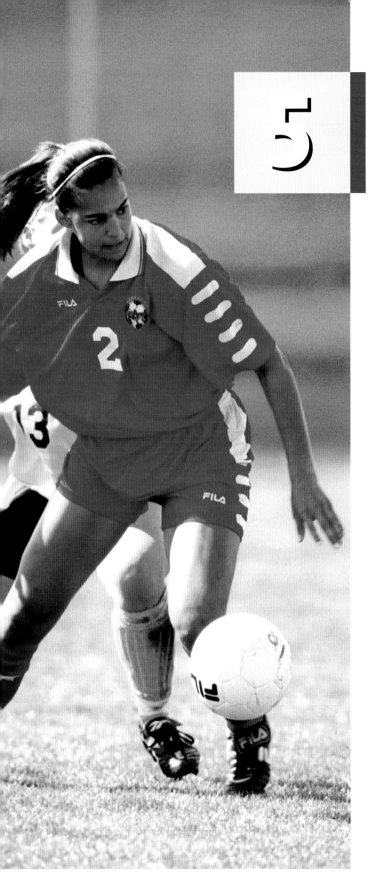

5

Defending Set Pieces

An organized attacking team can put pressure on their opponents by placing players in preplanned areas of the field. The attacking team knows what is about to happen; the defending team can only simply react.

The defending team must be organized in all possible free-kick situations. In this chapter we will lay down some basic principles to help you organize your team defensively. The defending team must have the discipline and concentration to deal successfully with defensive free kicks. If a single defending player forgets to stay alert or reacts slowly, it can lead to the team's giving up a goal.

Free-Kick Defense in Middle Third

When a free kick is awarded in the middle third of the field, the defending team must be ready to deal with two different situations: 1) a long direct or diagonal pass into the defending third of the field; or 2) a short, quick, free kick.

Defending players around the ball must maintain concentration on the play and remain active, not prepared to stop, so as to deal with any short free kick. The best ways to deal with this situation are: 1) Coach players not be too quick to turn their back to the ball and retreat down the field. Have the nearest players retreat slowly with their eyes on the ball and on the attacking players around the ball. 2) Have an equal number of defenders take positions around the ball as attacking players. This will also help make the attacking free kick more predictable for the rest of the defending team.

Next, the back players, with the help of the goal-keeper, must establish the line of defense. The depth of their line may vary, depending on the abilities of the players in the team, the physical abilities of the opposing players, and how much time is left on the clock. The biggest concern is making sure the ball is not played in behind the defense!

Free Kick Defense in Defending Third

When a free kick is given in the defending third, in or around the penalty box, the defending team must quickly organize to defend it.

The first thing the defending team must decide is how to defend this situation. Does the free kick require a wall? Does the free kick not require a wall? Should the team defend the free kick like a corner?

Free kicks that do not require a wall are usually taken from central areas of the field and are too far away from the penalty box, at a distance of 30–35 yards, or from wide positions of the same distance. The defending team should not place a wall any farther than the top of the penalty box.

When the free kick is central, the last line of defense should be no deeper than the penalty spot and probably no higher than the penalty box. The defending team should also not let the ball quickly be played wide for an early cross-in behind the defense or allow the ball carrier to penetrate on the dribble and then cross the ball into the penalty box.

When the free kick is wide and does not require a wall, the last line of defense will depend on how wide and how close to the goal line the free kick is located. If the attacking team puts more than one player on the ball the defending team must match this. This will stop passes being played down the flanks and allowing crosses to be played in behind the defenders holding the line in front of the goalkeeper.

The goalkeeper must help take responsibility in establishing the last line of defense. The coach, considering the players, must decide if they are going to defend by space-marking, man-marking, or a combination of both. The coach can use the field markings to help the team establish the last line of defense. For example, a free kick that is in a very wide position ten yards or less from the goal line could be defended as a corner. The defenders would use the six-yard box as a guide to establish the last line of defense.

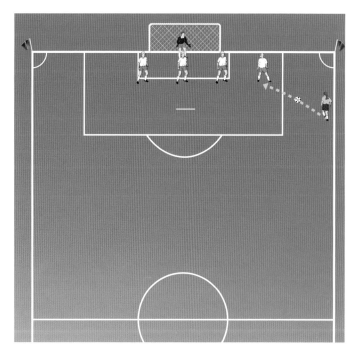

wide position, 6-yard box — last line of defense

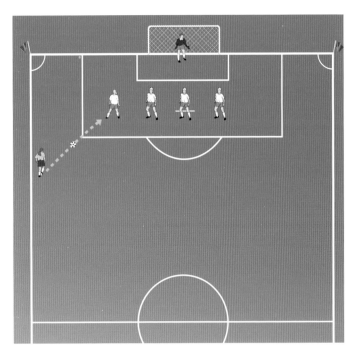

penalty spot — last line of defense

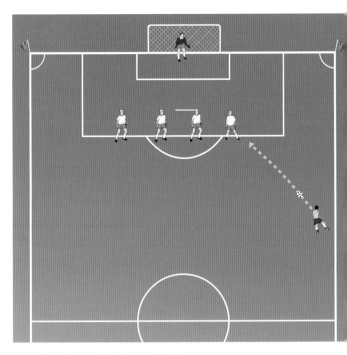

top of the box — last line of defense

We highly recommend space-marking the near-post space because it's difficult for the goalkeeper to get to that area of the field should the ball be driven there.

Setting the Wall

When a free kick is given around or inside the penalty box, the defending team must quickly organize and set up the wall. This is done by considering two questions:

1) *Who determines how many players go into the wall?*

This solution needs to be worked out on the training field. But, to answer the question, the goalkeeper will determine how many players go into the wall. The ability of the goalkeeper and the level at which your team participates will also play a big part in the number of players in the wall. Who

goes into the wall should also be predetermined. At the college level, for example, where you have somewhat free substitutions, we recommend this predetermination be done by position. If a new player comes on, she should know if she belongs in the wall or not. If the free kick is awarded on the defending team right-hand side and the goalkeeper calls for two players, it's always the right-side midfield and next central midfield player. If the call is for three players, it's the far right-hand side and the two central midfield players. If the call is four, then it's all four midfielders. If the call is five, then one of the two forwards is added.

2) *Who lines up the wall?*

Again, this is determined pregame. We prefer that one of the strikers have the responsibility to line up the wall, allowing the goalkeeper to be ready for a quick shot on goal. It is also that player's responsibility to make sure that the wall is organized by height, from high to low, from the near post. The player on the near post needs to have

lining-up wall

the near post on the inside shoulder to make sure the ball is not bent around to the near-post space.

After this player lines up the wall, she now becomes what we call the window player. This player positions herself in line of the far post and the ball, thus creating a window for the goalkeeper to see. If it is an indirect free kick, then the window player must charge the ball to help block the shot.

The positioning of the goalkeeper should always be as central as possible. A problem we had with our goalkeeping was that if the wall had to have four to five players and was just at the right angle it really forced our goalkeeper too far from the center of the goal. The adjustment we made was to have the end player on the inside of the wall take a half step from the wall, making a small window. This allowed our goalkeeper to see the ball and be positioned in the center of the goal.

In the 1986 World Cup in Mexico, a tactic that the West Germans used was the jumping wall. They would jump straight up in the air to increase the height of the wall. I found out later that, if the kicker took a long, straight approach, the wall would not jump. If the kicker's approach was a very oblique one, or a slice, then the wall would jump. In the women's game, I have found this a very useful tactic to stop shots, and also to help out the goalkeeper. This tactic will likely take a good amount of practice, in order for the wall to correctly time the jump.

Indirect Free Kick inside the Penalty Box

An indirect free kick inside the penalty box is not that frequent an occurrence. However, your team must be ready should it happen. In such a case, you will have to deal with either of two situations: 1) an infraction occurring where you can organize a wall, or 2) a wall organized on the goal line because there's not enough space between the goal line and the ball.

Defending Throw-Ins

When defending throw-ins, players should be prepared to do four things: 1) keep up concentration; 2) move into marking positions early, while the ball is out of play; 3) mark players, including the thrower, tight in the area of the throw-in and in all areas of the field; and 4) apply pressure to the intended receiver of the throw-in.

When defending long throw-ins, the defending team needs to mark the target player front and back, and be first to the ball. The other defenders must be aware of their marks and track runners who run off the target player.

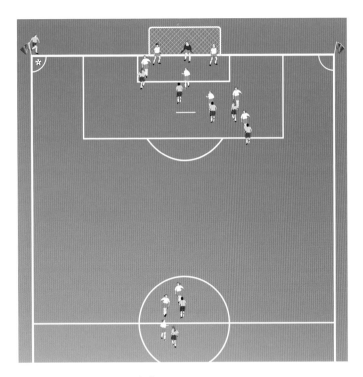

man-to-man defense

Defending Corner Kicks

The first question the coach must resolve is in setting up the defense. There are three ways for a team to defend: 1) zonal, 2) man-to-man, and 3) a combination of both. Whatever is decided, there are certain principles that do not change.

When a team is defending a corner kick, the goalkeeper should direct the defending team. The major threat from the corner is an inswinging ball to the front half of the goal. If the goalkeeper positions herself too far away from the near post, she runs the risk of not getting to the ball first. She also may have her path obstructed by both defending and attacking players. The goalkeeper should take up position no farther than halfway from the near post, with her body facing outward. This way, she is able to attack the ball and is in good position to handle any balls to the far post.

A defender who defends at the near post should be overlapping the near post so that balls don't squeeze in between the defending player and the near post.

In the modern game, some teams don't place a defender at the far post. Our professional opinion is that it still makes sense to place a player in that position. The player should be positioned inside the far post, facing out, so she can see the whole field. The far-post player should be deep enough so she can see the kicker through the side netting at the near post.

Zonal Defense

When defending in a zonal, the whole formation is built on the principle that the defenders must attack the ball and are responsible for the space in front and, in the example shown, to their right.

The first consideration is whether the defending team should place a defender ten yards from the kicker. The reasons for this possibility are: 1) the defender is an obstruction that the kicker must play around and over; and 2) to have a defender out to deal with a short corner.

Four players are positioned across the six-yard box. It is very important to have a player at the near post to deal with service driven there. Two players are also positioned on either side of the penalty spot. Their marking responsibilities are the same as the four. These players are also responsible for any corner that is played back to any late runners.

The next question is whether to keep one defending player high. This should make the attacking team keep at least two players back, and also provide an outlet for a quick counterattack should the ball be cleared by the defending team. If the defending team decides to bring all their players back to defend the corner kick, then this player should join the other two players to make three along the penalty spot.

If the attacking team does play a short corner, the player defending the near post must go out to make two. The player defending the far post moves to the near post. The player's movement to the near post must be behind the goalkeeper, so

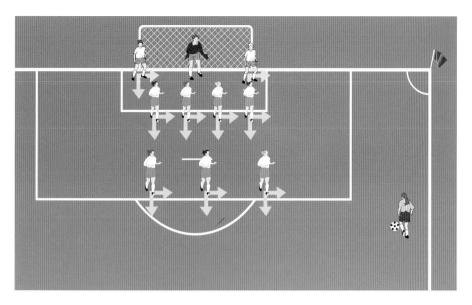

zonal defending

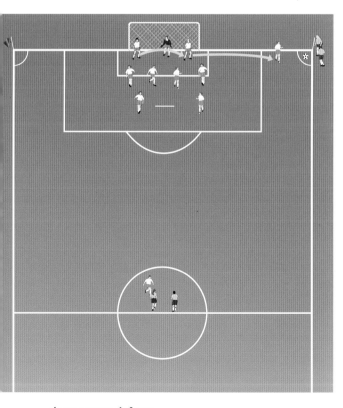

short-corner defense

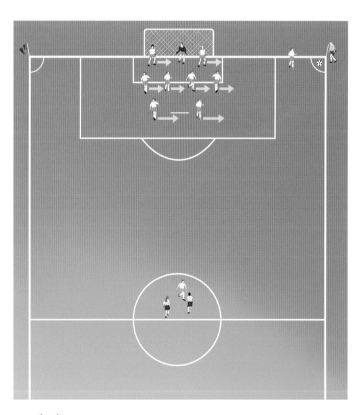

zonal adjust

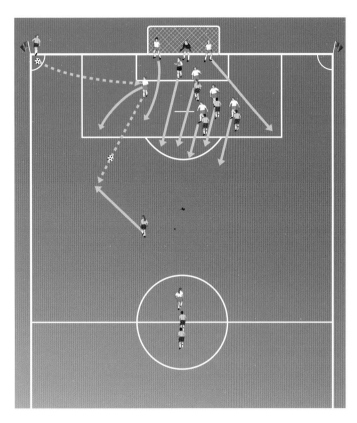

push-out defense

the goalkeeper's path to the ball is not impeded.

The two players must keep the ball in front of them and not allow the service into the box.

Pushing Out

When the ball is cleared from the corner, the defending team must clear the penalty box quickly. The nearest defender must get to and close down the ball. The rest of the defenders should push to the ball and close down the spaces. The only player who does not push towards the ball is the player who is at the back post. This player should come out at an angle away from the near post and mark the area at the back post.

6

Pressing Soccer

Pressing in soccer can be compared to basketball's version of full-court pressure, and some type of half-court trapping style of play. To be successful, the coach must instill the correct mental attitude before he/she can get the team to press. In the women's game, we have found pressing to be very effective because of the different levels of strength, power, and speed as compared to men. These differences will allow, if players are coached correctly, the women's team to squeeze the space even tighter.

Advantages of a Pressing Attitude

- It fits the American mentality of going forward, not sitting back—instant gratification.
- Other American sports—American football, basketball, baseball, hockey—are high scoring games compared to soccer. By pressing, you automatically raise your chances to score goals!
- All-out attack is what the American public likes to see. Sports are still part of the entertainment business.

- When the ball is lost, there is immediate motivation to switch modes and try to win it back.
- Players learn to play the risks, while being alert to counterattacks.

The choice of where to press is influenced by three things: 1) the strength of the forwards; 2) the strength of the opponent; and 3) the game situation, such as being a goal down.

The Formation

Before examining the pressing style of play, here is some information regarding the formation or "loose framework" that most top clubs operate.

- The system is usually a lopsided version of 4-4-2, with one of the wide midfield players being a deep-lying winger while the other wide midfield player has strong, attacking tendencies.
- Zone defense is used by the back three or four players.
- Mobile twin strikers who relate well to each other are an important feature of the structure.
- Hardworking, skillful central midfield players link the whole unit together.
- Key players offer leadership to the group, usually in the back.
- The skillful implementation of width, depth, and interchange (diagonally and back-to-front) are prerequisite to successful possession and penetration play.

Ingredients of the Pressing Game

We can view the pressing game under the three headings:

Pressure • Possession • Penetration

Pressure

When the opponent has the ball, the aim is to reacquire it without delay.

Pressure on the Ball   The nearest player to the ball "closes down" the player in possession. Applying tight and constant pressure will force the opponent's head down, turning to the short pass or dribbling. Try and channel the opponent into a crowded area to create a double team. The strikers only comply with this in the attacking third of the field if they have adequate support.

Leadership is an important factor if the group's efforts are to be synchronized. The team must have a clear understanding of when they are going to press the ball as a unit.

Marking Opponents   Opponents who are in close support of the player with the ball must be picked up. All marking must be goal-side and ball-side for interceptions. The player stands off her opponent slightly and entices a pass to her opposite number. The defender sprints the final few yards to intercept the pass! Midfield players have to move across to the area in which the ball is located. The front player on the opposite side from the ball drops in to cover. Defenders far from the ball may be required to mark two players.

Squeezing the Space   The back four do not permit large gaps to appear between them and the midfield. The depth and cover deteriorate the farther the defenders are from the ball. When the ball is on one wing, the defending fullback on the opposite side will be in line with the central defender nearest to her or slightly ahead. The goalkeeper must be prepared to act as a sweeper. Offside is a by-product of this arrangement.

Possession

By playing "pressing soccer," a team inevitably finds itself in tight situations, either having just recovered the ball or having opponents trapped in their own half of the field. Players are, therefore, required to be proficient in these tight, stressful situations. A sensitive touch, both in dribbling and passing, and tactical awareness are vital if players are to retain possession of the ball and penetrate the opposition. Midfield players, in particular, must be knowledgeable about angles of support. Front players must work hard at creating as much depth as possible in an attack in order to maximize the play space available to the team. Change of pace and direction by front players, and wide play—involving overlapping or direct running—are all necessary ploys calculated to create space and the options necessary for a successful attack. In the pressing type of play, efficient passing is the key that opens all doors.

Penetration

Shortest Path   When the ball has just been won, the shortest path to the goal should always be the first priority.

Wide Play   When faced with a crowded or low-pressuring defense, the use of the wide areas becomes vital. Play the ball infield and then out, giving the wide player space in which to operate, or look for a quick switch of play in order to leave the wide player 1 v 1.

One-Two Combinations

Combinations are vitally important, particularly on the edge of the penalty box when the opposition is tightly packed. Players should be acutely aware of the play possibilities that come from a one-two situation:

- The player on the ball drives forward and feints to play one-two.
- The one-two pass is played off the wall player.
- The wall player turns and moves off, feinting the wall pass.
- The wall player plays the ball out to a "third player," creating a three-man combination.

Key Coaching Points

- The appropriate weight, timing, and angle of the pass are vital.
- The ball moves before the wall player in order to bring her marker out of covering position.
- The player who initiates the move must use a change of pace in order to bypass her marker.

Second-Striker Play   Twin strikers work to create deep, narrow situations for the midfield players to exploit. One striker comes short, while the other pushes forward. The ball is played to the farthest striker, thus producing greater penetration from midfield passes. The striker who has come short then peels off and supports her striking partner. The ability of the twin strikers to relate to each other cannot be overstressed. Good chemistry and communication are "a must."

Power Shooting   The ability to shoot from outside the penalty box is important when the opposing players are being pushed back and create a congested area in front of the goal. This type of shooting spells danger for two reasons. First, the goal area can be so congested that the defending goalkeeper, often screened of shots, cannot react in time. Second, deflections can be created and the ball's unpredictable path almost impossible to defend against.

Additional Factors

Fitness   Only players of supreme fitness can possibly hope to play the pressing game. Endurance capacity, however, is not enough—they must combine this with speed, particularly over short distances, and with flexibility of movement.

Coachability   The player who is unwilling to do her part in the team effort and who only plays when she has the ball is a liability in this type of game. The player must be willing, sometimes, to forego any personal glory for the good of the team. The coach's role of coordinator must be accepted by all.

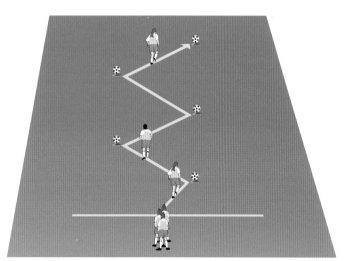

station slalom

pressing 6 v 3

Player Mentality In the pressing game, players must be prepared to work incessantly, but, even more important, they must have the capacity to concentrate and to react positively and immediately to new situations.

Leadership Leadership is a necessary ingredient in any successful operation. Key players must take responsibility for initiating and carrying out the pressing plan. Players must be prepared to take up another colleague's role in order to avoid a possible collapse of the team structure. Communication of a tactical or motivational nature means the players help to coordinate the team's movements, thus avoiding a breakdown through their collective effort.

Professional Foul Pressing also means fouling to stop the opposition's attacking moves, when the press has been beaten.

Station Slalom Exercise

To set the mentality of pressing, the players, on command of the coach, move from station to station, moving their feet as if in the midst of a game. They move all the way through the slalom, practicing their moves. In turn or various rounds, the moves could include:

- Pressing the ball. Players' feet move outward, as if trying to block the pass or shot.
- A slide tackle.
- Pressing the ball, "showing" an imaginary attacker on the inside or outside.
- Pressing the ball, with a pressuring and covering player.

Key Coaching Points
- Get quickly to the ball.
- Don't dive in.

pressing 8 v 4

pressing 8 v 6

Pressing Practices

6 v 3

Three teams of three players in 20-by-20 grid. One team defends while the other two join forces and try to keep possession of the ball. When a defending player intercepts the ball, her whole team changes from defending to keeping possession. Likewise, the player who gives the ball away is joined by her two teammates in the middle, i.e., defending role.

8 v 4

In 30-by-30 grid the aim in this exercise is to press the ball. Two teams of eight. One team of eight plays possession soccer, the other team, using only four players at a time, defends. After one minute the defending team replaces the players who have been in action with their four rested players.

If emphasizing possession play the result is decided by passing efficiency; e.g., ten passes equals one goal. If emphasizing defending skills, the number of interceptions is recorded.

8 v 6

This is a small-sided half-field game that highlights zone pressing and creates matchlike stress on the five when they are in possession. Each team has a goalkeeper. One team has seven players on the field, the other five players. The team with seven players can only play two-touch; the team with five players plays freely and are the ones doing the pressing.

pressing 8 v 8

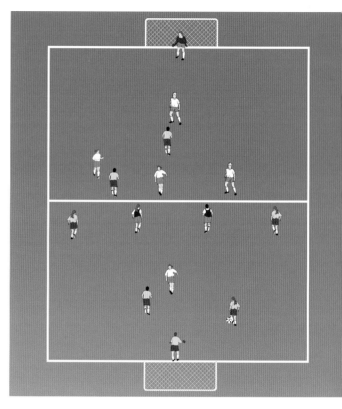

pressing 9 v 6

8 v 8

This half-field game stresses man-for-man pressing. Both teams have a goalkeeper and seven outfield players. A normal game is played except that defending players must operate a strict man-for-man defensive system. The coach may add a center line so the team can also work on playing with offsides.

9 v 6

On a 70-yard-long field this is a small-sided game that highlights pressing the individual. The team with nine players nominates two playmaking players. These players must be clearly identifiable to both teams. The team with nine players must play through either of these two playmakers before their team can score. The playmakers are restricted to two-touch play. The defense must try to put pressure on these two playmakers when the ball is in their area.

7

Offsides

When considering the offside tactic, the team needs an understanding of why and how to apply it. The biggest reason to apply the offside tactic is to reacquire the ball. The defenders must attack the ball at the same time to stop any penetration passes. If the attacker tries to dribble through the pressure, the defenders should win the ball by sheer numbers.

It is not recommended to execute this offside tactic high up in the defensive third, because the space is too great for the goalkeeper to control. So it is recommended to use it in the defensive third of the field only for:

• Clearance of long balls and crosses into the central areas of the field. Clearing the ball into these areas allows the defending team to get imminent pressure on the ball with numbers because the distance for them to cover is shorter and there should already be a concentrated number of players in that area. The coach needs to show the players that if the ball is cleared into wide positions it is not recommended to try to play offsides. Again, because of the lack of numbers in that area and the distance to cover to get there to apply pressure, by beating one defending player the attacker can beat the whole team.

equal-number drop back

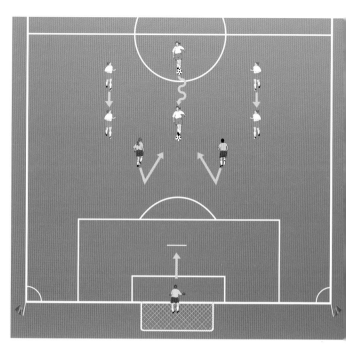

lesser-number drop back

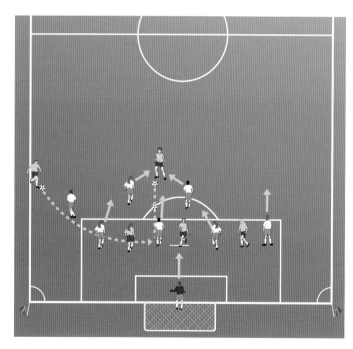

long-ball clearance

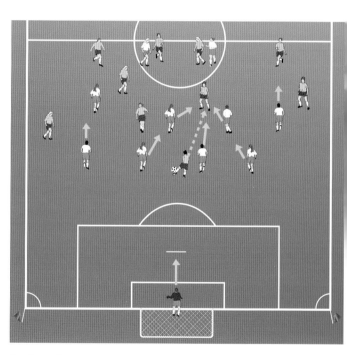

backward pass pressure

- Clearance in central areas after a free kick or corner kick.
- When a forward makes a back pass with the goal at her back. Immediate pressure on the backward pass is required. This will force the receiver to play quickly either forward or wide. This tactic is used to set the player who made the back pass offsides, because she will more than likely be ball-watching.

Beating the Offside Trap

If we agree that, to be effective in setting the offside trap, the defending team needs to apply pressure to the ball as they push out, then, to beat the trap, the player in possession must recognize when there is incorrect coordination between the two movements. She must recognize this and understand how to beat the trap.

There are four ways the attacking team can defeat the trap:

Dribbling Through   The player who is in possession has time to control the ball and get positive forward momentum toward the defending team as they push out. If the player in possession is not quick enough to penetrate the entire defensive line, she will at least draw players toward her. This will create spaces behind the first defender for other attackers, too, which creates time and space to run at them.

Passing Through   Again, the problem starts when the trapping team does not apply enough pressure to the ball quickly enough. The player who is in possession has time to control, get her head up, and find a runner and space where the ball can be played to.

The run can come from another area of the field, from a player whose starting position is deeper then the player who is in possession of the ball. This movement is a push-pull movement on the striker's runback towards the halfway line. At the same time, the runner (usually a midfielder or defender) from the deep position runs forward. The pass can be made on the ground, which is the easiest to control, or a short diagonal chip with backspin, which will hold the ball up as it bounces.

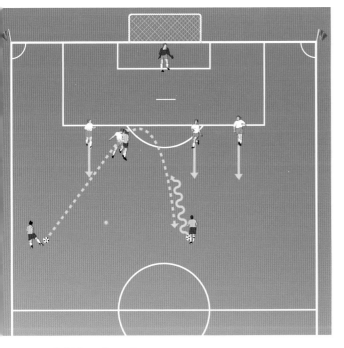

dribbling through

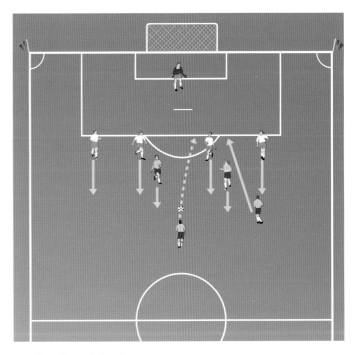

passing through (push-pull)

passing through (parallel run)

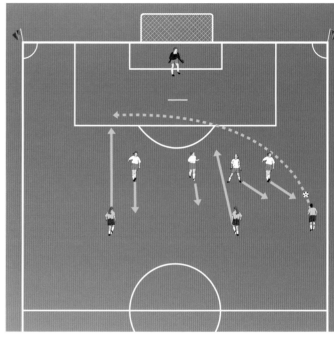

diagonal pass

A through pass can also beat a trap when the attacking strikers run parallel to the defending line and one looks to time her run as the ball is played, then darts behind the defending line. A runner can also starts from a wide position and runs inside.

Diagonal Pass   A short or long diagonal pass is another effective way to beat the offside trap. The first example is when the ball is in a wide position and the defending team tries to push out and press the ball. The biggest mistake is that the defending team tries to trap when the ball is in a wide position, where usually there is not a large concentration of defending players and runners can run vertical to get behind the defending team.

With a long diagonal switch, the ball can be played over the top of the defense to an attacking player who is starting her run from deep and arriving late. For example, an outside back who is getting forward.

Two Passes   Here you need two passers to beat the trap. The ball is cleared out and pressure is applied. Pressure is applied to the ball quickly, but not quickly enough to stop a square pass to a teammate, who then plays a penetrating pass in behind the defending team who is pushing out.

Self Pass   In an old-fashioned version of up and over, the player in possession beats the trap by playing the ball to herself, a self pass. A situation may occur when the ball is cleared out and the ball may be bouncing and the attacking player will volley the ball over the top of the defending team as they are pushing out.

In all of these examples on how to beat the trap, the common dominator is that there is not enough pressure put on the ball; either amount of pressure by itself or number of players getting to put pressure on the ball. The defending team, also, does not push out quickly enough or at the right time.

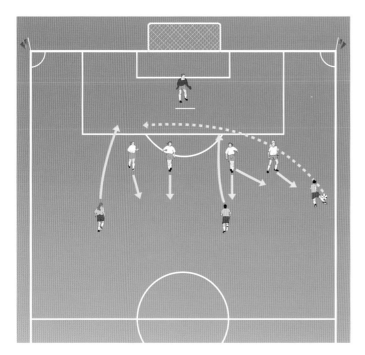

over-the-top long diagonal

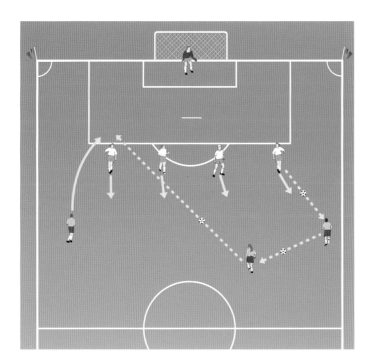

two passes (square)

8

Counter-attacking

At the highest level of the women's game, as teams have become better organized, defensive in-blocks and less pressing up the field have encouraged counterattacking, either in a specific situation or as a main strategy. As teams become more difficult to break down, counterattacking—requiring space, speed, and direction—will become an essential part of every team's repertoire.

Three Keys to Counterattacking

How
- Must create space to play into by dropping off.
- Must have at least one high player to quickly play into.
- Must demonstrate patience when defending.
- Must create space by intelligent running off the ball in the middle and attacking third of the field. When attacking players are sprinting forward they need to run in narrow spaces, making it harder for the defending team to cover more than one attacker.

- Must be done at speed.
- Must be done with directness in running and passing.
- Breaking the offsides trap.

Where

- Possession won through run of play
- Pressing
- Off defending corners
- Off defending free kicks
- From wide positions; crosses
- From goalkeeper distribution; punts, throws

When

- Once possession is won, quick decision to counterattack or to play possession.
- Play to space or feet.
- For space, long diagonal pass behind the defense. Must get supporting players into the box.
- Feet must get forward to support ball for passing combination, such as one-twos and up-back, through movements.
- Running with the ball into open space (midfield area). When to hold and when to pass. Supporting players running ahead of the ball into attacking spaces.
- Long-range shooting.

Advantages

- Does not fit the American mentality: teams are not used to playing against well-organized counterattacking teams.
- Low-risk defending, marking space directly in front of goal
- Conserve energy
- Potential to frustrate the opposition
- Goal-scoring chances from minimal passing movements

Disadvantages

- Does not fit the American mentality: not instant gratification oriented.

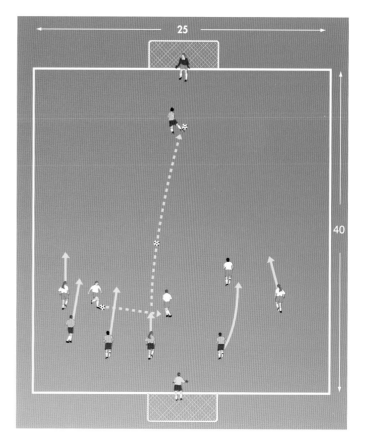

5 v 5

- Goes against the current American sporting culture. Hard to get American players to sit back and wait.
- Very situational—hard to teach.
- Must be very psychologically strong to be under so much attacking pressure for long periods of time.

Counterattacking Practices

5 v 5 on two goals with goalkeepers
Team in possession attacks with 5, while other team defends with 4 and a target player remains up front.

If defenders intercept, they must play to the target player and play combinations because the target player is not allowed to score.

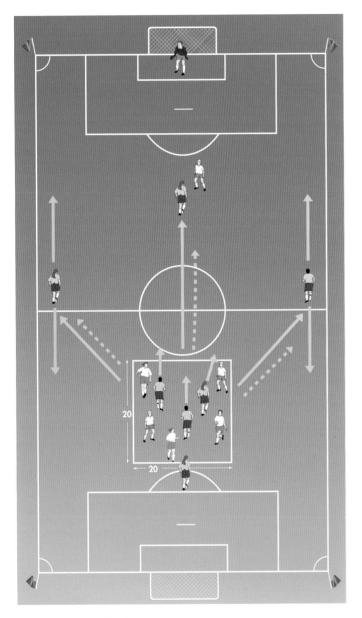

6 v 3 + 3 v 1

8 v 8 + 2

6 v 3 + 3 v 1

Team of three attempts to gain possession from six. Six have limited touches.

When the three win the ball, they counter to one support player who plays forward to the wingers or to the central striker.

8 v 8 + 2

With three goals, team X attacks one goal, while team O attacks two goals. Team O must have all players past offside line.

Encourage quick passes into depth and width after regaining the ball, use of free spaces on the wings, and quick transition.

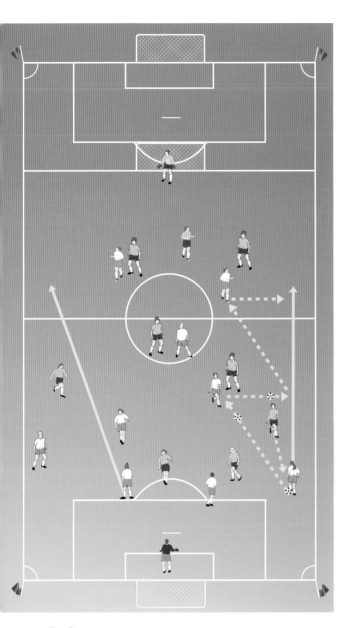

9 v 9 / 7 v 6 + 2 v 3

Each team has 15 minutes as the attacking team, two strikers; and 15 minutes as counterattacking team, three defenders.

The ball must be passed across the center line. When the ball is played to one of the strikers, two players from the attacking team can enter the attacking area to offer support.

When the defenders win the ball, they must immediately counterattack before the supporting players return to their starting position.

No offsides. Scoring, normal.

9 v 9

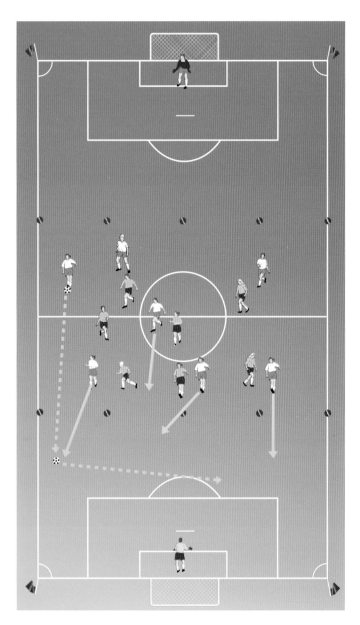

7 v 7

Concept is playing on the counterattack. In this game of possession, 5 passes equals one goal.

On the signal, team in possession attacks the goal to score. Opponents just have to defend goal. When the game breaks down, rest and walk back to the middle third of field.

Two goals for five passes—one goal if goalkeeper is beaten. All players have to be onside in attacking area.

7 v 7

Counterattacking

Playmaking and the Attack Switch

Every team has some type of playmaker, a player who tries to dictate the rhythm and tempo of play during the course of the match. In most teams, this player is positioned somewhere in central midfield. However, with more teams defending deeper, closer to their own goal, the player performing this role can also be a central back or sweeper. After all, this is where the free space is in which to operate.

Training the Playmaker

6 v 6 + 2 playmakers (warm-up)
Each group of six must find their playmaker and pass and support these players.

5 v 3 + 1 playmaker
In a 30 by 25 area. The five attacking players and the one playmaker try to possess the ball from the three defenders. If the three defenders win the ball they try to possess the ball and dribble out of the grid for a point. This element helps with the principle of play of transition.

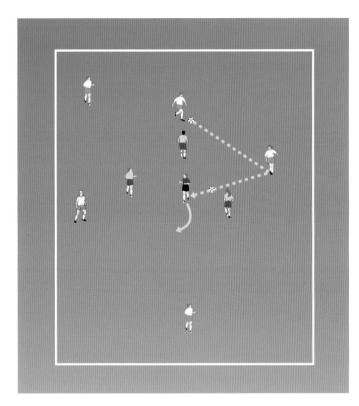

5 v 3 + 1 playmaker

5 v 5 + 1 playmaker + 2 targets

5 v 3 + 1 Restrictions

- The five attacking players have only two touches. This forces the playmaker to seek the ball out and support the players in possession.
- The playmaker has only one touch. This forces the five attacking players to support playmaker.
- The playmaker cannot play the ball directly back to the player who just passed her the ball. This helps develop combination play.

5 v 5 + 1 playmaker + two targets

The playmaker plays for both teams in a quarter of the field. Adding two targets to the training gives the practice direction. This exercise will help define the attacking and defending roles of the players.

7 v 7 + 2 playmakers

In area 18 by 18, full width. Playmaker plays with both teams. The coach must work on the relationship of the two playmakers.

9 v 9 + 2 playmakers

Full game—playmakers play with both teams.

Playmaker Coaching Points

- Do not chase the ball.
- Get free by going away to come back to the ball.
- Body position sideways on, so can see more of field. This also puts playmaker in a position to play the ball forward first time.
- Change the point of attack.
- Combination play—through 1-2s and 1-3s, third-man running movements.

Switching Point of Attack

When working with your team, get them to swiftly change the point of attack, or "play where they're not." This sounds easy on the surface but, when it has to be put it into practice, suddenly it becomes much more difficult.

The coach must first recognize why it is impor-

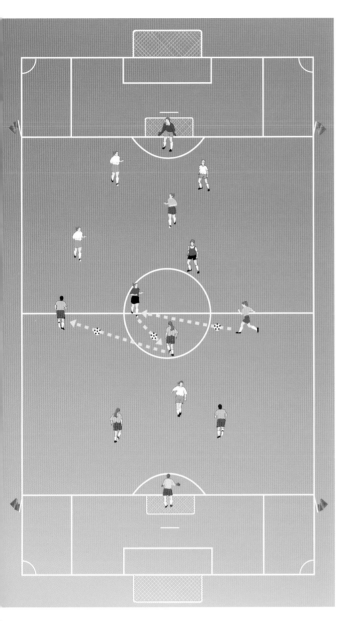

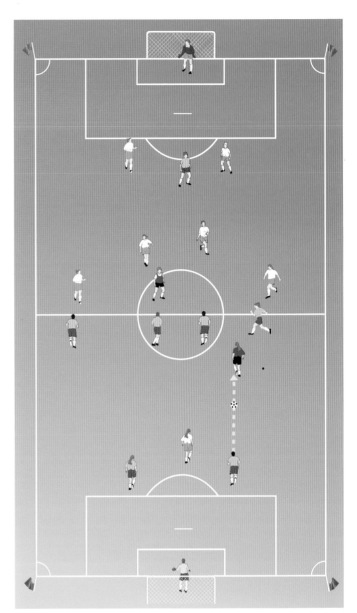

7 v 7 + 2 playmakers

9 v 9 + 2 playmakers

tant to change the point of attack. In changing the point of attack, the attacking team is trying to play the ball to a teammate who has time and space. This switch will force the defending team to move and re-establish a new defending restraining line. As the players have become better physically, and teams as a whole are more organized in group- and team-defending, switching has become increasingly important in moving the defensive

block. The next question is, "When will this tactic be necessary?" When the opposition is pressing the ball in their attacking third, or in their middle-field third, and when defending teams play low pressure and drop off, that's the time to switch the point of attack. Finally, you will want to switch the point of attack when the attacking team is counter-ing. This switching will help to change the rhythm of the game as well.

Coaching the Change

Here are some examples on how to train your team on changing point of attack.

3 v 3 v 3 / 6 v 3

In this quarter-field exercise the coach wants to establish certain principles. One, before you can change the point of attack, the team must establish a point of attack. The attacking team maintaining possession of the ball does this. Important concepts are: body position, see the whole field, and short and long support, the angle and distance of this support. The priorities of passing: a) penetration to feet or space, b) change point of attack, and c) possession passing. Also, there is the timing of the runs in relation to the passes. The visual cues to this are "head up," of the player who is in possession;"show," from the receiver;: and "pass." You need to also instruct your players not to kill the ball when controlling it. You want to keep the ball moving so the opposition has to keep moving as well.

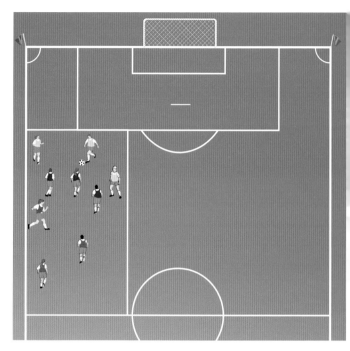

3 v 3 v 3

9 v 6

On a half field, the eight field players plus one goalkeeper defend the one large goal and attack to two small goals. When the six win the ball they try to score in the large goal. The coach now works with the eight players on all of those concepts, which you trained in the 3 v 3 v 3 / 6 v 3 but now the game has direction to it.

9 v 6

9 v 9

9 v 9 + 1 neutral

Playing box to box, coach all the coaching points, but a neutral player plays for both teams.

10

Crossing

A good defending team tries to keep the attacking team from penetrating their defense, either pushing them into wide positions or into central positions. If the attacking team is being pushed into wide positions, crossing the ball into the penalty box becomes a very important tactic to score goals.

There are three primary target areas that the attacking team should try to find: the near post, the middle of the goal, and the far post. Before the server crosses the ball, she must take into consideration three tactical elements: the space available, and the positions of defending and attacking players.

The crosser has technical and tactical considerations when executing a cross. As the crosser is dribbling down the touchline, she must be able to look up and see where the defending players are, including the goalkeeper. This is very important because the crosser is coached to serve the ball into open spaces. It's the responsibility of the runner to get into those open spaces. This will change if the cross is played from the end line, where the crosser will look for attacking players rather than spaces in which to play. The next consideration is getting the crosser to recognize where to cross the ball. If the defending team is not balanced and organized, the cross is played to the near post. If the defending team is balanced and organized, the ball is played to the far post. That cross will force the defending team to turn, and find the ball and attacking players.

As the crosser is running down the field, she must scan the field in-between touches on the ball. Visual cues that the crosser is about to cross the ball are a long last touch, a long leg stride, and the crosser's head going down. This will help the forwards to time their runs into the box. If the crosser pushes the ball straight down the touchline, the plant foot is placed towards the goal and must turn her body to cross the ball. However, this is very hard, especially running at full speed under pressure. A problem occurs when the player does not get all the way around the ball because the crossing player has planted herself to cross the ball. The ball rolls away from the crosser, making her cross her body with her leg. There is no approach angle for the crosser, and many times she ends up slicing the cross behind the goal.

If time allows, teach your players to touch the ball slightly inside towards the goal. This will provide an approach angle to the ball for the crosser.

Near Post

The target area that the crosser tries to find is on the edge of the six-yard box even with or slightly ahead of the near post. The runner should wait until the last possible second before sprinting into this space. If for some reason the attacking player runs into the near post too early, then she must either continue her run and vacate this space so it will open up again, or the attacking player can also back out of this space, and then run back into this space.

The near-post runner should look to run into the space at a 40-degree angle, which will allow a positive approach angle to the cross. The runner should also time her run so she arrives late but at speed and she attacks the space at the same time the ball does. When striking the ball, the attacker should look to redirect the ball and play the ball back from where it came. Also, if possible, the ball should be redirected in a downward path, again making it a harder shot for the goalkeeper to save. The speed of the runner and the speed of the cross will usually be enough to beat the goalkeeper.

Another option is to let the near-post runner either flick or dummy the ball and so that it crosses the face of the goal. This runner must then turn and frame the goal to be ready for any shot that is played back across the face of the goal.

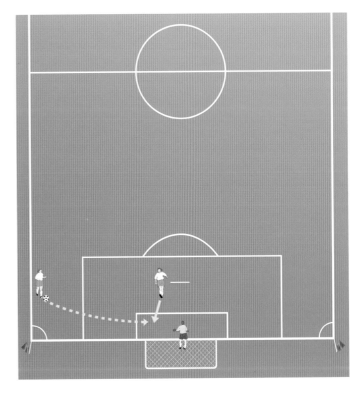

near post

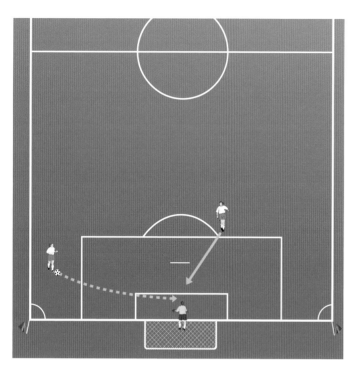

middle goal

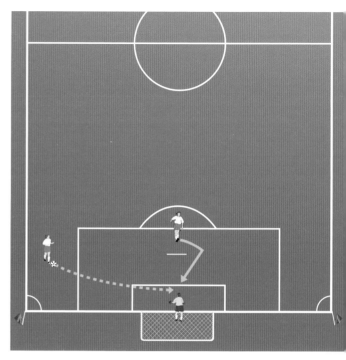

middle-goal feint

Middle of the Goal

The target area for the middle of the goal cross is around the penalty spot. If the cross is too far to the inside of the penalty spot, the goalkeeper should win possession of the ball. The problem with this cross is finding time and space in that area of the penalty box. One way to create time and space is to drag marking defenders beyond the near post. Or, hold the attacking position at the far post, keeping the middle of the goal area open for late arriving runners to that space.

A third way is if the attacking player can start her run in the target area and make a run to the far post, dragging the defenders out of the target-area space and creating the space for the attacking player to run back into.

This target area is not the best for crosses. This cross does not take any defenders out of the game because the ball stays in front of most of them.

Far Post

The target area is behind the far post. The depth of the cross should depend largely on the position of the goalkeeper. The crosser and the far-post runner should be aware of each other's position so the runner can make her run accordingly.

If the server is 20 to 30 yards from the touch-line, the cross should be played over the defenders into the space behind them. Should the crosser be farther out, the goalkeeper will be more central in her goal. The cross needs to be played beyond the six-yard box. Not many goals will be scored directly from this cross; therefore, heading or volleying the ball back across the face of goal will create scoring opportunities for teammates. The ball should be played behind the line of defenders, who must turn and react. With defenders turning and trying to find the ball, there is always the possibility of the attacking player's losing her marker.

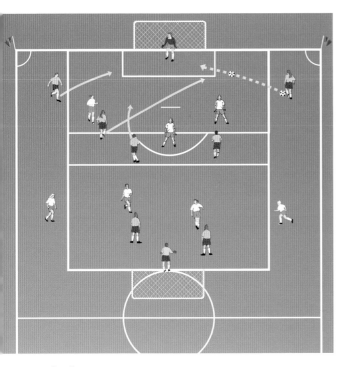

8 v 8

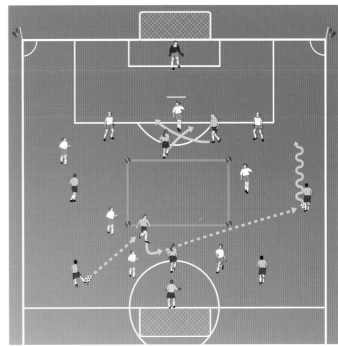

no pass-through

The run to the far post is a wide bent run. This runner should arrive late and at speed, without turning her back to the cross. Also, by making a bent run will help keep the ball in front of her and not let the ball go over her head. This will also allow the runner to react more easily by going forward and not backwards.

8 v 8 Cross   Goals are scored by shooting from outside the penalty area or after a cross from one of the wingers. The wingers stay outside the line. They can only come inside the field when there is a cross from the other side. Wingers have only one or two touches and the goalkeepers can only play to the winger following a back pass.

No Pass-Through   The coach lays out a 15-by-20-yard grid in the middle of the field. The players have to pass the ball around the grid, but may run through the grid to get forward.

Attacking Set Pieces

FREE KICKS

Defending Third

The first consideration for all attacking teams when they have a free kick in their own defending third of the field is safety! To avoid giving away any stupid goals. The next consideration is, can the free kick be played quickly and directly to get behind the defense? If that is not a consideration then, can the ball be played quick and short to maintain possession of the ball? Finally, can the ball be switched and played wide to get around and behind the opposition?

Middle Third

When the attacking team has been awarded a free kick in this part of the field, the first question is, can the attacking team punish the defending team if they loose concentration by playing the ball quickly and directly to get behind the defense? If this is not available, can the ball be switched to try to get around and behind the opposition? Finally, the ball

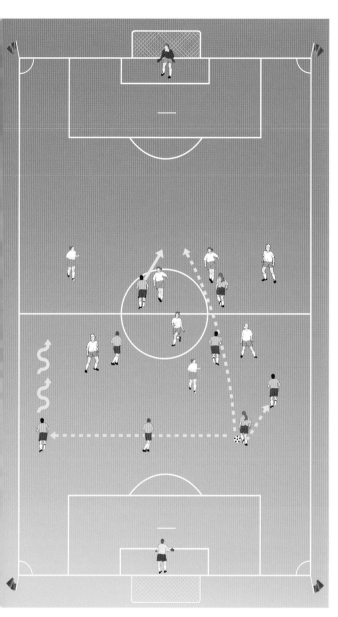

defending third

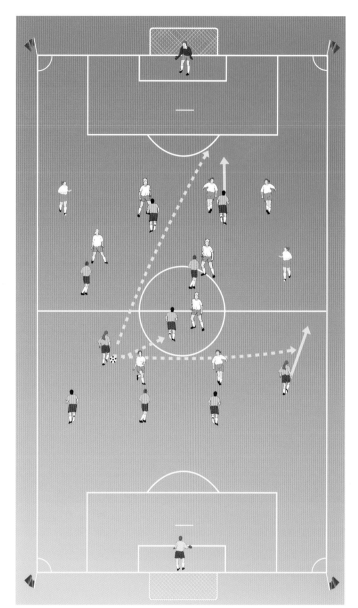

middle third

can always be played short and quickly, but maintaining *possession* of the ball has to be a priority.

Attacking Third

When the attacking team has been given a free kick in the central area of the field and too far away for a direct shot on goal, then the attacking team should play at an angle which helps create a natur-al attack angle. The attacking team should take three things into consideration. Can the ball be played into the far-post space? This service needs to be deep enough to get behind the defense and at an angle that will help create a natural attack angle for the attacking players. If short, the defending team can counterattack on this poor service. Next, has the defending team dropped off too much, allowing the attacking team to play short and attack the space in front of the defense?

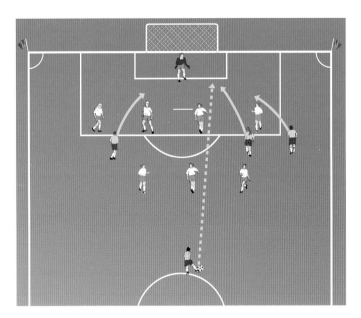

attacking third

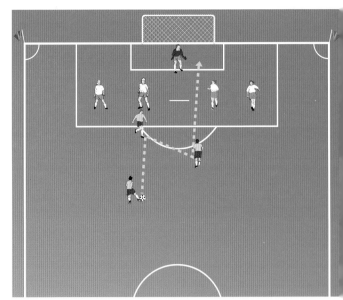

central free kick

Also, can the ball be played wide to get behind the defense and allow a cross to be played between the defense and the goalkeeper?

Central Goal Shot)

When a team is awarded a free kick within direct shooting distance (30 yards or less), the attacking team has the advantage over the defending team by being able to place players in predetermined places on and around the ball.

In getting a team organized on the practice field, the coach must consider a few key points.

Key Coaching Points

- Keep the free kick simple; don't set up the team for failure by asking them to play too many passes when a direct shot might be the best option.
- A coach must look at his/her players to see who is accurate, and who can strike the ball with power.
- Stay cool, and pick the right option.
- Remain organized in the back (attacking team should ask themselves, what if?).
- Follow-up, for rebounds.

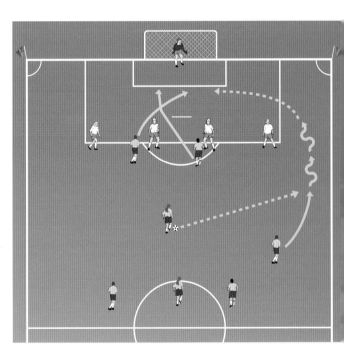

free-kick option

With indirect free kicks, the law has been changed to where the ball only has to be touched, and it's not required that the ball roll a full circumference before it can be played by another player. This law change has simplified indirect free kicks.

Wide Positions

When a free kick is awarded from a wide position, it will pose some questions for the defending team. Do we use a wall? If so, how many? How high does the rest of the team hold the defending line?

The attacking team must practice how they are going to attack the defense from this position.

A driven, inswinging ball to the near post, to the center of the goal area is a very difficult ball to handle for the defending team. A missed clearance by the defending player can result in a goal as well.

The rest of the attacking players should try to do two things: 1) attack certain spaces, and 2) get goal-side of the players who are marking them. This ball to the near-post space can be flicked on to the back post, for players who are running into those spaces as well.

An outswinging ball can be played to the back-post space. However, the service must be played deep enough so the attacking team cannot be countered.

Inside Penalty Box

When a free kick has been given inside the penalty box, the attacking team will probably have to beat all 11 defenders to score a goal. If the free kick is less than 10 yards, then the defending team will build a human wall. To beat this human wall, there are several points to remember:

- Attacking players need to stay calm.
- If the ball is at a narrow angle, the first touch should widen the angle to the inside of the goal. With the ball being played to the inside to widen the angle, there will be more goal to shoot at. If the ball is to be moved, then the ball must be played away from the goal and not square.
- If the free kick is more centralized, play the first touch-back away from the goal. This gives the shooter more time and space, and the ball coming towards the shooter is much easier to strike and to get into the air than the ball that runs across the face of the shooter.
- Aim high and away from the goalkeeper.

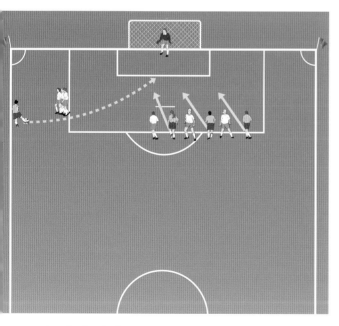

inswinging ball

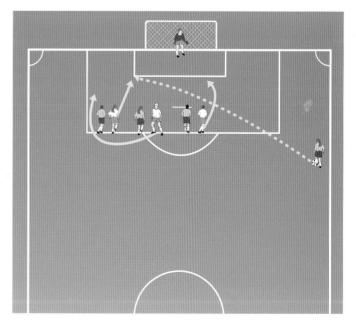

outswinging ball

PENALTY KICK

A penalty kick is awarded when a foul that otherwise would have resulted in a direct free kick is committed within the penalty box. The attacking team is awarded a direct free kick from the penalty spot, which is 12 yards from the goal. A goal should be scored every time. It looks so easy, which is the reason why it's hard for some players.

ATTACKING CORNERS

When planning for attacking corner kicks, the coach needs to consider three important points: 1) decide whether to use an inswinging or an outswinging corner.; 2) decide whether to attack the near- or far-post areas; and 3) choose the attacking players carefully for the required jobs, with the server being first and foremost!

Inswinging Corner Kick

The inswinging corner kick has advantages and disadvantages. One advantage is it applies great pressure to the defending team and the goalkeeper. In most cases, this ball is driven, making it hard to clear. Also, with the ball bending towards the goal, there is always the possibility of the ball going straight in or attacking players redirecting the ball in. There is also always a chance of a goal being scored because of a missed defensive clearance.

With an inswinging corner, in many cases the ball is driven to the near-post area. This service should be delivered at head height. The reason is that if the ball ends up at the back-post area, either by the ball being flicked on or missed, the ball will still be playable.

If the ball is played to the near post it puts great pressure on the goalkeeper. Her decision on whether to stay or come for the ball to catch or clear has to be made quickly.

We recommend placing an attacking player in front of the goalkeeper to impede her vision and path to the ball.

The inswinger cornering to the far post is looking to deliver the ball to the back of the six-yard box. The first priority is for the attacker to score; if not, the ball needs to be played back across the face of the goal. The runner who makes runs to the near-post areas, should look to frame the goal. Framing is when the ball is played past her. She then would turn and face the goal.

One of the disadvantages to the inswinging corner kick is it puts pressure on the server to be very accurate with the service. Another disadvantage is when the ball is played in towards the goal the path of the ball makes it easier to be cleared by the defender.

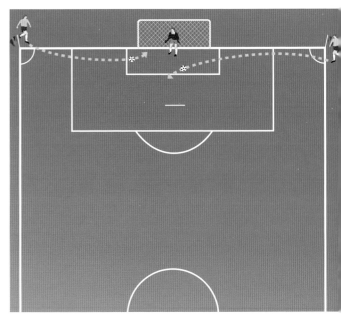

corner kicks

Outswinging Corner Kick

This corner has many advantages. For one, this type of service can fool the goalkeeper. She picks up the line of the ball; then starts to commit herself, only to have the ball bend away from her at the last moment.

When the ball is bending away from the goal, it is also bending into the path of the oncoming attacking players. This makes it easier for the players on the attack to strike the ball at goal. An attacking player can also use the pace of the ball in her favor to gain power for the shot on goal.

The server has the option of playing the ball to either the near or far post, thus giving the attacking team two target areas.

If the service is too high it will give the defending team time to adjust and to attack the cross. If the service is played between the penalty spot and the top of the box and is too high it could put the defending team into an all out attack off the clearance.

However, it has two disadvantages. The first is that any immediate chance of the ball going straight into the goal is lost, as is the possibility of the ball hitting a defending player and going in. The second is that, since the goalkeeper may not have to handle any crosses, it eliminates any chance of the goalkeeper making a mistake.

Short Corner

The attacking team will use a short corner either to have the serve taken closer to the goal and at a wider angle or to get a shot on goal. When using a short corner, remember that the 10-yard rule will allow the attacking team to place two players on the ball and keep any defending players away from the ball until it has been played. After the attacking player plays the ball to her teammates, she must then get out of an offside position and behind the ball.

The attacking player who has possession of the ball must attack the defense by going down the line towards the goal.

When the defending team reacts and challenges the attacking player with the ball, it draws defending players out of the danger area. This creates time and space for the attacking team. When the attacking player is challenged, she will attempt to pass the ball back to the attacking player who originally played the ball. This player will now look to serve the ball. On a narrow field, the short corner can be used to get a shot on goal.

If a corner is on the right, the attacking team will try to have a left-footed player serve or shoot the ball. The opposite applies on the left attacking side: have a right-footed player serve or shoot the ball. Surprise is the key.

ATTACKING THROW-INS

At any level of soccer, there will be more attacking throw-ins than any other type of set piece. During these throw-ins the defending players tend to relax and lose concentration and should be punished.

In general, there are five major points to remember, whether the throw-in occurs in the defending third, middle third, or attacking third:

- Take the throw-in as quickly as possible.
- Look for the farthest unmarked player. Remember, you cannot be in an offside position when receiving the ball directly.
- If not the farthest unmarked player, find the nearest unmarked player. She will have time and space to play the ball back to the thrower or to initiate an attack herself.

- Make the throw-in easy for the receiver to control. Do not throw the ball short, where it bounces into the receiver. This makes it even harder to predict where it may bounce.
- The thrower must get back into the game as quickly as possible.

Back Third

Because of where this throw-in takes place, the tactical priority should be safety first. The ball should be thrown in to an unmarked player, including the goalkeeper, who can either play it back to the thrower or switch the ball to the other side of the field to play out.

If the thrower wants the ball to be played back to her first time, then the ball should be thrown to either her head or foot.

Finally, if neither of the first two options will work, simply throwing the ball up the line will relieve the pressure and possibly gain ground for another throw-in.

Middle Third

When you have a throw-in in the middle third of the field, your team can take a few more chances. Here are two: 1) a throw-in to an unmarked player who can maintain possession, and 2) a long throw-in into the attacking third of the field to a runner who has "shown" to the ball and then spins up the line, or to a striker farther up the field.

The marking of the receiver who comes back for the ball along the touchline will usually be goal-side and ball-side, which will leave the space down the line open.

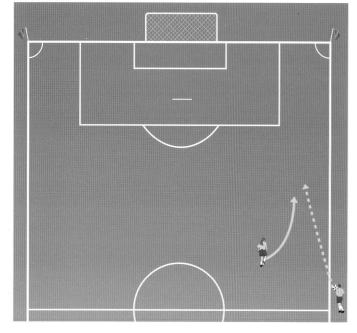

middle third throw-in

Attacking Third

In the attacking third of the field a quick easy throw-in is the best option. The more people included, the greater the chance of failure. In this third, you'll notice many teams doing the same things: 1) 2 v 1, to keep possession or to attempt to get in a cross; 2) some type of cross over; 3) scissors; and 4) a long throw-in.

2 v 1 When trying to execute a 2 v 1 throw-in in the attacking third, it's very important for the thrower to adjust her position quickly to give a good angle for the ball played back, an angle so the one defender cannot mark both attacking players at the same time. Also, this angle will allow for a first-time cross into the penalty box.

Crossover Move The attacking team needs to remember that there are no offsides on throw-ins, so the defending team will have to mark players and will do this by a man-to-man system. The trick here is to create the space by running players out of a certain space, followed by other attacking players running into the open spaces. The critical thing here is the timing of the runs so attacking players are not caught standing in those spaces waiting on the ball to be delivered.

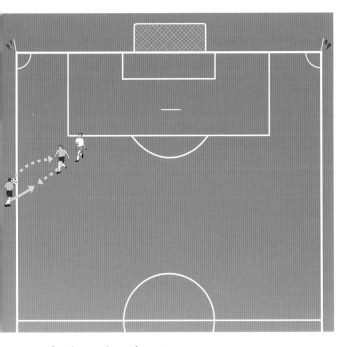

2 v 1 attacking throw-in

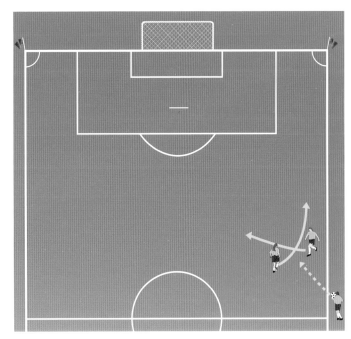

crossover move

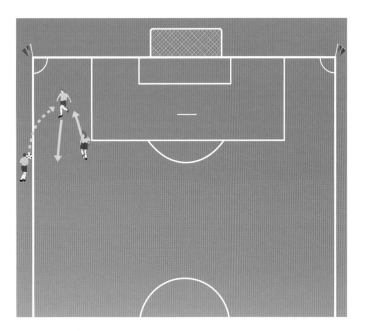

scissor move

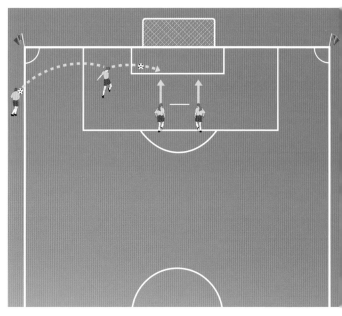

throw-in to flick

Scissors This is where two players will stand one in front of the other, then fake in the opposite direction and run in the other direction to lose their mark to receive the ball. This also creates a 3 v 2 situation which will help to maintain possession.

Long Throw-In When putting this throw-in into the attack, the coach first must find a player who can throw the ball at least 35–40 yards. Next, the throw needs to have as straight a trajectory as possible, making it easier for the target player to flick, and redirect on. The target player needs to be a good header of the ball and be able to handle front and back marking. The coach needs to organize runners off the target player looking for the flick.

When practicing set pieces, it's important that a coach make sure not to ask players to perform tasks that they are not able to perform. This will lead to failure and frustration during the match. A coach must also allocate training time to practicing all the team's set pieces.

Free-Kick Games

With limited training time, most coaches don't schedule much time to practice free kicks. However, depending on how you try to develop free kicks, it can be very static and boring; especially when the weather is bad. Another problem is roster limitation, if a team only has 16 to 20 players; there's not enough for a full scrimmage. A coach, however, can organize a half to three-quarter field game of 10 v 5, 6, 7—whatever the numbers are.

The ten attack the big goal, trying to score a goal. The smaller team defends the big goal and tries to score in one of the counter-attack goals. The coach can award attacking free kicks and corners by stopping the action at his/her discretion, or upon a successful number of passes. The coach can flip-flop the attack and defense, and work on defending set pieces.

free-kick game

12

Goalkeeping

The goalkeeper is considered one of the most important players on the field. They are the last line of defense and the only players allowed to use their hands. These two elements make goalkeeping a highly specialized and crucial component of the game.

Coaching the Position

Goalkeeping isn't just about catching a ball and blocking shots; today's goalkeepers need to be proficient in using their feet, communicating with the defense, and generating attack through distribution and quick organization.

Technical   Regardless of the technical skill being executed by the goalkeeper, the number one priority is to get her body behind the ball. The goalkeeper should always err on the side of safety, and be sure to provide the biggest barrier between the ball and the goal.

Set Position   The goalkeeper's feet should be placed shoulder-width apart, with knees slightly bent to bring the body weight forward onto the

set position

front part of the feet. The arms and hands should be outside the line of the body, and waist high. This is the proper position for a goalkeeper prior to fielding any type of shot.

Angle Play   A goalkeeper makes the goal smaller by using angle play. Pretend there is a ball placed 18 yards out. Draw an imaginary line from each post to that ball. The triangle formed denotes the angle within which an opponent must shoot the ball in order for it to go in the goal. If the goalkeeper stands on her line and does not move, the ball has approximately 4 yards of space to the right and left of the goalkeeper to go into the goal. As the goalkeeper moves forward, off her line, the yardage will decrease, thereby cutting down the angle. The same is true if the ball is moved to the side of the goal. The triangle's shape changes and becomes oblong. The goalkeeper should find the center mark between the posts and move straight towards the ball, cutting down the angle. On wide-angle shots, the goalkeeper, erring on the side of safety, should "cheat" slightly towards the near post.

angle play

ground scoop

Working on Technique

Ground Balls (scoop catch)

The scoop catch technique should be used on rolling or lightly bouncing shots. The ball is allowed to roll up hands and trapped against chest.

Key Coaching Points
- Body behind the ball
- Hands behind the ball
- Head over the ball, with eyes on the ball
- Keep legs together to present a barrier in case of a catching error
- Position hands openly, so ball will roll into hands and curl up into forearms and chest

Common Faults
- Reaching for the ball with hands or feet without moving the body
- Head up, and eyes off the ball
- Legs spread too wide

Ground Balls (dive or front smother)

This technique should be used on driven ground balls or bouncing balls coming at a faster pace. It's also a common technique used during poor weather conditions that may cause the ball to bounce unpredictably.

Key Coaching Points

- Very important that entire body be directly behind the ball.
- Keep head in position over the ball, and eyes on the ball.
- Shoulders should be square towards the ball and hands behind the ball, with palms facing outward.
- Arms are outstretched to meet the ball before hands and forearms pin the ball into the chest.
- Push off with the legs in a forward motion, landing on the forearms with legs extended behind.

Common Faults

- Not squaring up behind the ball, resulting in a deflection of the shot rather than catching.
- Not pinning the ball into the chest before landing on the ground.
- Forearms spread too wide, resulting in the chest landing on the ball or the ball skipping underneath the body.

Waist-High Shots (scoop catch)

This technique is similar to the ground-scoop catch; however, the ball will be caught between the knees and the chest.

Key Coaching Points

- Body is directly behind the ball.
- Arms are outstretched with palms facing up.
- The same scooping motion as the ground catch; the body should give with the ball.
- Pin the ball to chest with forearms and hands.

Common Faults

- Body is not squared-up directly behind the ball.
- Trying to catch with the "W" —forcing the ball down instead of in.
- One arm is placed under the ball while the other is placed over the ball.
- Goalkeeper's arms, hands, or body is stiff and rigid, and does not allow the necessary "give" to the ball.

waist-high scoop

high catch

Chest-High Shots ("W" catch)

This technique is used when dealing with shots that are chest-high or above.

Key Coaching Points

- Hands are in "W" shape; thumbs do not touch.
- Hands are on top half of the ball.
- Fingertips must take the brunt of the shot, while palms control the ball.
- Arms should reach for the ball, then "give" with the ball as it is being caught.

Common Faults

- Hands are on either side of the ball (thumbs too far apart); ball goes through the hands.
- Hands are on the bottom half of the ball; ball is deflected behind goalkeeper.
- Hands and arms are rigid; ball bounces off hands.

Catching High Balls

This technique is used when balls are driven above the head.

Key Coaching Points

- One-footed take off; bring one knee up to chest.
- Fully extend the arms, with the hands forming the "W" shape.
- Catch the ball in front of the body at its highest point.
- Bring ball in to chest to protect it.

Common Faults

- Faults are same as chest-high shots.
- Catching the ball directly beneath or behind the body, which results in a lack of balance when landing.
- Catching the ball too low, this results in the opponent's being first to the ball.

Parrying Balls over the Bar

This technique is used for balls that are too high to catch cleanly but are, nonetheless, on goal.

Key Coaching Points

- Goalkeeper determines where the ball is going and opens her hips in that direction.
- Using the crossoverstep, the goalkeeper gets underneath the ball.
- Using the power step, the goalkeeper reaches for the ball with the hand that is opposite the post the ball is nearest to.
- Reach for the ball at the point where it dips to the crossbar.
- Hand should be kept open and stiff; palm should redirect the ball over the bar.
- The chest should always be open to the field of play.

Common Faults

- Goalkeeper backpedals to the ball; this takes too long and makes it difficult to incorporate the power step.
- The wrong hand is used, causing the power step to be off. Ultimately less height is reached in the jump.
- The goalkeeper reaches for the ball while it is still ascending, and misses it entirely.
- The fingertips hit the ball, or the goalkeeper only slaps at it and the ball is not redirected.
- With chest turned toward goal, the hand ends up pushing the ball into the goal instead of over the bar.

parrying

Handwork Drills

- Server stands over goalkeeper and throws ball down at goalkeeper's face, 50–100 times.
- Server stands 10–12 yards out and shoots at the goalkeeper, who must handle cleanly—no drops or bobbles. Play to three points. If the goalkeeper handles cleanly, she gets a point; if she drops or bobbles ball she loses a point. Drive the shots.
- Two servers work the one goalkeeper. The goalkeeper is in goal and the servers alternate throwing the ball to the goalkeeper, who plays "hot potato."
- The goalkeeper closes her eyes and the server tosses the ball into her outstretched hands. Goalkeeper must feel for the ball, then catch.
- Server holds the ball and goalkeeper places hands about two inches above, in the proper "W" style. Server, at random, drops the ball, and goalkeeper must catch it before it hits the ground.

- Goalkeeper sits in front of the goal while the server stands 6 yards away and punts ball at the goalkeeper. This can be done 10–30 times, varying the intensity of the shot. The goalkeeper should be instructed to use only her arms.

Airwork Drills

Parrying Warm-Ups   Goalkeeper is 2–3 yards off goal line. Server throws balls, alternating the sides over goalkeeper's head. Goalkeeper must parry it over the crossbar, 20 times. The idea is goalkeeper should use drop step, and power dive, and opposite hand to opposite post.

Backtrack Drill   Goalkeeper starts on goal line. Server has 12 balls about 12 yards out. Goalkeeper must jog out and touch the ball. The server throws ball over goalkeeper's head while they are backtracking to the goal. Goalkeeper parries ball over, or must power dive to save the ball.

handwork drill

Increasing Range   Server is about 18 yards out with a pile of balls. Goalkeeper is on goal line. Server punts ball into 18-yard box and goalkeeper must come off line and save in the air before ball bounces. Can do this drill with no pressure or with pressure (add forwards).

Redirecting 1   Two servers stand 20 yards apart with a goalkeeper closer to one server. The closest server throws ball over goalkeeper's head and the goalkeeper must get to and redirect ball to other server using fist.

Redirecting 2   Server is at one post with goalkeeper. Goalkeeper is squatting down and server tosses ball to the far post. Goalkeeper must get up and redirect the ball to the sideline.

Crosses   Goalkeeper can be given balls with or without pressure.

Two-Keeper War   Two goalkeepers are standing near one another. Server throws ball up between them and they must save cleanly for a point (game is to three points).

They are allowed to push, shove or interfere with each other in any way to make other goalkeeper drop the ball.

Team Trains the Goalkeeper   Any type of small-sided game focusing on crosses into the box will allow for repetition. The field players will be training on how to finish crosses or clear defensively from a cross, while the goalkeepers will be working on decision making and technical skills of catching crosses.

Shot-Stopping and Reaction Drills

Superman   Goalkeeper is on her stomach in goal, facing server. Server yells "Go!" Goalkeeper must get up and save thrown ball, 10–12 balls or for a specified time.

Turn Catch   Goalkeeper faces the goal. Server 12–18 yards out has balls and yells "Turn!" Goalkeeper must turn and save shot, 20–25 shots.

Wall Drill   Goalkeeper stands about 2 yards away from a wall. Server stands behind, and tosses ball over goalkeeper's shoulders. Goalkeeper must react to deflection off the wall, 30–50 balls.

Lateral Quickness   Goalkeeper starts at post; cone is set up $1/2$–$3/4$ of the goal. Server stands about 10 yards out, and calls out "Go." Goalkeeper must leave the post, and make the save from the server's dropkick. The idea is for the goalkeeper to make the save on her feet; no dive unless it is necessary.

Somersault Shots   Goalkeeper performs a somersault toward the server. As the goalkeeper gets to her feet, the server shoots.

Interference Reactions
1) Goalkeeper has short cones placed randomly in front of her. Server shoots balls at the cones, and goalkeeper must react to their deflection.
2) Two players are jogging about 6 yards out in front of the goalkeeper in goal. Server shoots balls in to players, and they get in the way or redirect the ball. Goalkeeper must react.
3) One goalkeeper is in goal, one goalkeeper is standing 5 yards in front of the other goalkeeper. Server throws the balls to the head of the foremost goalkeeper, who deflects the ball. Goalkeeper in goal must react and make a save.

Quick Shot   A line of ten balls is in place about 10 yards out. Goalkeeper is about 5 yards away from balls. Server shoots balls about 1–2 yards out of goalkeeper's reach and the goalkeeper must react.

Footwork

The footwork of a goalkeeper will be the determining factor in getting the body behind the ball for all types of save.

Shuffle Step

This is used when the goalkeeper is in the set position and may not be sure where the ball is being shot. It is typically an adjustment-type of step when dealing with angle play, especially when the goalkeeper is getting reset for a ball that has been moved to the side. It is the slowest type of footwork for goalkeepers, but it's the easiest to use to get back into set position the quickest.

 **Key Coaching Points**
- Stay low, keep knees bent, chest over the knees
- Feet do not cross; one foot steps wide and the other follows but does not touch

 **Common Faults**
- The goalkeeper is upright.
- Feet either hit each other while moving, or crossover of feet occurs.

Crossover Step

This is used when the goalkeeper knows exactly where the ball is going. It is the fastest way to get to a ball.

crossover step

Key Coaching Points
- Goalkeeper must know to which side of the goal the ball has been shot, or if it is going high.
- One leg crosses straight over the other. If the ball is shot to her right side, the goalkeeper must cross her left leg over her right, and vice versa.

Common Fault
- Goalkeeper guesses wrong and crosses over to wrong side; ball is shot in the other direction.

Power Step

This is the last step taken before reaching for a ball that requires a power dive, parry over the crossbar, or redirection of a cross.

Key Coaching Points
- The leg closest to the ball pushes off the ground in a springing motion.
- The opposite leg's knee drives in an upward motion, swinging the hips to a tilt and lifting the butt.

- The opposite leg does not cross over the other.
- The use of the arms will increase the momentum and drive of the power step; they work simultaneously with the legs.

Common Faults
- The leg opposite the ball is the leg to push off the ground.
- The leg opposite the ball does not get driven in an upward motion. This keeps the hips and butt low and therefore the leap is not high or far.
- The arms do not help propel the jump.

Diving

Collapse Diving

Diving for a ball from a close-range shot. There's not enough time to shuffle to it. It's typically a ball that is also shot relatively close to the goalkeeper's body, so she simply collapses onto it.

Key Coaching Points
- Stay low with weight on front of feet, chest forward.
- Leg closest to the post nearest the ball will collapse behind the other leg.
- Both legs come out from under body and body shoots downward quickly.
- Body should be barrier between goal and ball.
- Hands should catch ball in "W" shape.

Common Faults
- Goalkeeper tries to shoot legs forward and misses the angle on the ball
- Goalkeeper lands on her elbow, trying to catch the ball

Low/Medium Ball Diving

Diving for balls that are shot below the waist/chest.

low-ball save

power diving

Key Coaching Points

- Stay low with weight on balls of feet, chest forward
- Select either crossover, shuffle, or combination of both to get body/hands behind ball
- With leg closest to the ball, step 45 degrees to ball, push off ground, reach for ball with hands in the "W"
- Catch ball and land on the ground; hands should be in the "W" on the ball
- Body should stay square to the field of play the entire time

Common Faults

- Not using footwork to get behind ball; just a "falling over" movement
- Using leg farthest from ball as last step, resulting in weak momentum towards ball
- Placing elbow to ground to break the dive; the "W" comes apart
- Not stepping "to" the ball therefore not as much goal being covered
- Turning and landing on stomach. Painful, and the dive can never reach full extension or power

Power Diving

Diving for balls hit above the waist/chest.

Key Coaching Points

- Footwork must get towards ball with some momentum
- Last step to ball is the power step
- Arm opposite to ball must be thrust across face in same moment opposite knee is being driven upward in the power step
- Reach for ball in "W" catch and receive ball
- Find point on ground to place the ball, which will land first and take the brunt of the landing
- The rest of the body follows and the goalkeeper can lessen the impact of the landing once the ball has hit the ground by rolling out of dive (body must first land, then the roll begins)

Common Faults

- Goalkeeper power dives for a low or medium ball.
- Power step is not present, resulting in the body landing roughly and hips hitting ground first.
- Goalkeeper tries power step with leg opposite the ball as the pushing-off leg, resulting in no height to power dive.
- Goalkeeper's arm opposite to the ball does not get thrust across face: result is lack of height to dive.
- Goalkeeper tries to land by placing foot down at the same time as the ball.
- Goalkeeper tries to roll out of dive before she has entirely landed.

Diving Drills

Progression   Using 10–14 balls. There are three sets in this drill, going from post to post. All diving starts with low, then medium, then high (power) diving. Rest period is the time it takes the other goalkeeper to do the drill.

Over-Cones Parrying   Goalkeeper starts at one post and must dive over the cone at other post. The idea is to work on the extension of the body and parrying the ball with the palm. All 7–8 balls are served at the same post, then switch sides.

Power-Diving Warm-Ups   Standing with the ball in hands, the goalkeeper launches herself in the air and lands, buffering her weight on the ball. One goalkeeper is on her hands and knees (pony); the other goalkeeper is a step away from the pony and must clear the pony and receive a ball from a server. One goalkeeper holds ball at arm's length and the other goalkeeper must propel herself at the ball. The idea is to work on driving the opposite knee and arm.

Cone Drill   Goalkeeper starts at one post; at the opposite post eight cones are set upside down. Goalkeeper must cross over to the cones and flip one up, then make a save at the opposite post. Idea is to work on moving the goalkeeper forward in diving—to dive *to* the ball.

Pony Drills (plyometrics)   Same pony drill as before, except that the goalkeeper does a double knees-up over the pony, then dives back to the side she came from.

pony drill

Rapid Fire Server has 10–12 balls in a line at the 18 and starts by shooting a ball to the goalkeeper's side, attempting to make her dive. Shooter does not wait for the goalkeeper to get up from the save, but works down the line of balls.

Doubled Goalkeeping A line of twelve balls is at the top of the 18. One goalkeeper is on the goal line and another is 5 yards from the shooter. Shooter tries to shoot balls past first goalkeeper.

Grid Work No pressure: a grid of 20 by 20 feet has ten balls in it. The goalkeeper must make as many saves as she can in a specified time (one minute). Pressure: see breakaway drills.

Refrigerator Drill Goalkeeper starts at a post and must make a save (either a high- or low-thrown ball) at the other post. Then she must get up and run around the outside of the goal, come back to the post she just made the save at, and make a save at the opposite post, 6–10 balls.

Two-Person Diving Goalkeepers are at opposite posts; either work with two servers or one. One goalkeeper must double over the other (knees up) and one goalkeeper rolls under the other when they cross in the middle. The goalkeeper doing the roll receives a high ball she jumps for, and the goalkeeper who doubles must dive for her service. Then they switch (continual motion). If you don't have two servers, goalkeeper receiving high ball just touches crossbar.

"Go" Drill Goalkeeper must start at a post. Server has balls at feet about ten yards out. Server yells "Go" and goalkeeper must start out from post (using shuffle steps until she knows where ball is served). Server then chooses to serve in direction goalkeeper is moving, or in opposite direction.

Work on both posts. The idea is to help the goalkeeper with footwork and reaction.

Technical Work Goalkeeper faces opposite direction. Server says "Turn" and goalkeeper turns to the right; server gives ball in that direction. Idea is to work on taking 45-degree step *to* the ball. Alternate turning direction.

Accompanying practice is placing three cones out from the post. Goalkeeper works on diving to these "balls."

Rope Work Tie rope to a post and have one goalkeeper hold other end waist-high; other goalkeeper must dive over. Can make into a progression drill, having the goalkeeper receive ball at one post then make power-dive save over the rope.

As a warm-up drill, server holds rope and three balls are sitting on the ground about seven yards from each other all on one side. One goalkeeper holds ball in hands, and serves to other goalkeeper who makes power dive over the rope, then goes for a low-ball save, under the rope, to the sitting ball.

Somersault Shots Server stands with ten balls about 18 yards out, in a semicircle. Goalkeeper must make roll and, as she is coming out of the roll, the server shoots. The idea is to make the goalkeeper dive *to* the ball.

Breakaways

A type of breakaway, the smother save, occurs when the goalkeeper and the opponent meet the ball at the same time. Typically, it is seen when the opponent pushes the ball too far in front of her while dribbling on a breakaway.

breakaway

Key Coaching Points

- Stay low.
- Approach opponent every time ball is in front of them; at ball touch, be in set position.
- Dive to ball hands-first, when ball is touched too far away from foot of opponent and enough ground has been closed down.

- Hands and forearms should be in snakelike shape, and go directly at ball to smother it.
- Head is behind hands, off the ground.
- Legs follow momentum of dive, and follow-through on smother.
- Body makes a big barrier parallel to the goal behind.

Common Faults

- Runs out of goal out of control, missing opportunity to smother ball.
- Slides to ball feet-first instead of hands-first, losing the angle.
- Head is too high above hands, leaving goalkeeper prone to injury either from opponent's foot or knee.
- Body is shifted too perpendicular to goal; angle is lost.

Shot Save

This type of save occurs when an opponent breaks away and shoots before the goalkeeper can close enough ground between them to smother the ball.

Key Coaching Points

- Stay low.
- Approach opponents every time the ball is in front of them; when they touch the ball be in the set position.
- When opponent shoots the ball, goalkeeper must be set.
- React to which side ball was shot and collapse dive or power dive.

Common Faults

- Moving when opponent touches ball; ball is shot underneath goalkeeper.
- Prematurely going down into dive; opponent simply moves ball around goalkeeper.

Breakaway Drills

Warm-Up Goalkeeper starts about 10 yards away from second goalkeeper. One feeds ball to other goalkeeper, then chases after and smothers her shot. Ten times alternating sides. The idea is to go hands-first to ball and to stay low.

Push-Up Drill Two servers are 10 yards apart. One goalkeeper is in a push-up position in front of one of the servers (perpendicular). The server closest to the goalkeeper kicks ball under the goalkeeper to the other server, and the goalkeeper must get up and chase the ball and smother the shot. Ten times.

Mirror Drill Three balls are set up 5–7 yards apart. One goalkeeper is on one side of the line of balls and the other goalkeeper is on the other side of balls—the working goalkeeper must mirror or copy all movements of the other goalkeeper (if one goes to the right, so must the other). Then the goalkeeper goes at a ball and points at it and meets it the same time as the working goalkeeper. The idea is for the working goalkeeper to go hands-first and smother shots, and to go hands to near post. Eight times.

Drop Kicks Goalkeeper is in goal. Server, about 6–8 yards out, dropkicks ball at charging goalkeeper. (Server must call out "go" just before kicking ball for goalkeeper to react.) The idea is to elicit a reaction-type save, but also partially anticipation. This is good preparation for failed clearances off corners; the goalkeeper is basically throwing her body at the ball.

Grid Work Same grid work as in diving drills, same time. Server picks random balls and points at and meets the goalkeeper at the same time for smothered shots.

Goalkeeper Wars Set up a 20-yard grid. Two goalkeepers play 1 v 1 against each another with smaller cone goals.

Live Breakaways Goalkeepers make saves from field players from all angles.

Keep Away Select a field player with good ball control skills and play "keep away from the goalkeeper" in a small 15-by-15-yard grid. Goalkeeper gets point for saving or stealing ball from player's feet. Player gets point for dribbling under control to certain sides of the grid.

Distribution

Bowling Throw

When a goalkeeper has a teammate within 15 yards, this is a safe and usually very accurate way to distribute the ball. This type of throw is also the easiest for a field player to receive, because it should be rolling on the ground at the pace of a normal 15-yard pass.

Key Coaching Points
- Ball is cradled between the hand and forearm.
- Goalkeeper should step towards target.
- Ball should be released low to the ground so pass will remain on the ground when rolling.
- Ball should be placed in the space immediately in front of the player, so she can collect it instantly.
- Goalkeeper needs to follow the pass, and provide support

Common Faults
- Ball is released too high and it bounces to player, resulting in an even more difficult ball to receive
- Attempts bowling throw to players too far away; ball never reaches them, or pass is intercepted by opponent
- Ball is played behind or too far in front of the target player

bowling throw

Sling Throw

When a goalkeeper wants to distribute a ball directly to a teammate who is more than 20 yards away, the sling throw is ideal. It provides more power, gets to the target quicker and can be a great means in starting a counterattack.

Key Coaching Points

- The ball is cupped between the hand and forearm.
- The goalkeeper combines footwork with the throw, taking long powerful strides towards the target; the strides should continue once the ball is released.
- The arm is held straight down at the side. As the goalkeeper's foot opposite the side of the ball steps forward, the goalkeeper's arm comes around and over the shoulder in a quick, fluid motion.
- The ball is released when the arm is parallel to the ground, and it should be driven in the air with backspin.
- The pass should be in the space in front of the target; how far is determined by the positioning of the target and whether there is an opponent.

Common Faults

- The ball is not thrown directly over the shoulder but from the side of the body.
- No steps are involved in the throw; the pass loses power on release.
- The ball is released early and is projected upward instead of outward.
- The ball is released too late and is projected immediately into the ground.
- The ball is played behind or too far in front of the target.

1

2

sling throw

Punt

This distribution, along with a dropkick, will cover the longest distance in the shortest amount of time. Goalkeepers will use the punt to deliver the ball far up field to relieve pressure from the defensive third of the field. Unfortunately, this type

3

4

◢ Key Coaching Points

- The ball is held in the hand opposite the kicking foot.
- The goalkeeper takes steps forward with the last step being a longer stride with the leg opposite the kicking foot.
- The ball is dropped in front of the kicking foot.
- The foot should connect with the ball as the knee is over the ball.
- Strike the ball with ankle locked and the foot pointed down, using the laces.
- The knee snaps through the kick and the entire leg swings forward through the hip.
- Eyes should be on the ball when striking the ball.
- The goalkeeper should land on the kicking foot when following through.

◢ Common Faults

- The ball is held in the hand on the same side as the kicking foot.
- No steps are taken during the punt, losing power and distance.
- The goalkeeper's stride is not fluid (skips), losing power and distance.
- The ball is not hit off of the laces, causing punt to veer left or right.
- Lack of follow-through in kicking leg, loss of power and distance.
- Goalkeeper looks upfield when striking the ball, and doesn't connect with ball.

of distribution will result in a 50/50 ball and possession can be lost. A goalkeeper should make sure teammates are pushed upfield and the punt should be played to a target who can flick it on to a teammate. If done quickly, a punt is a great counterattacking tool when the opposing team has committed too many players forward.

dropkick

Dropkick

This is a more accurate long-distance pass that is, compared to a punt, easier for teammates to control. The dropkick has more backspin on it, and is favored in bad weather, such as wind or rain, because it is a more "driven" kick.

Key Coaching Points

- The ball is held in the hand opposite the kicking foot.
- The goalkeeper takes steps forward with the last step being a longer stride with the leg opposite the kicking foot.
- The ball is dropped in front of the kicking foot slightly in front of the body.
- The ball will hit the ground and as it comes up the goalkeeper will strike the ball.
- Strike the ball with ankle locked and the foot pointed down using the laces.

- The knee snaps through the kick and the entire leg swings forward through the hip.
- Eyes should be on the ball when striking the ball.
- The goalkeeper should land on the kicking foot when following through.

Common Faults

- The ball is held in the hand on the same side as the kicking foot.
- No steps are taken during the punt, losing power and distance.
- The goalkeeper's stride is not fluid (skips), losing power and distance.
- Goalkeeper hits the ball too soon, or waits too long as the ball is coming off the ground.
- The ball is not hit off the laces, causing the punt to veer left or right.
- Lack of follow-through in the kicking leg, loss of power and distance.
- Goalkeeper looks upfield when striking the ball, doesn't connect with ball.

Goal Kick

At the higher levels of competition, you will see more goalkeepers taking their own goal kicks. This is done for two reasons. The first is that the goalkeepers are much stronger and have greater distribution skills. Also, it is an advantage if all field players are in position as the kick is taken.

Key Coaching Points

- The approach to the ball is slightly angled with most of the body coming directly behind the ball.
- The ankle is locked and the foot downward and slightly bent.
- The last stride before the ball should be long, and the planted foot should be placed slightly behind and next to the ball, pointed in the direction of the kick.
- Strike the bottom half of the ball using the laces, as the leg swings forward through the hip.
- Eyes should be on the ball.
- The goalkeeper should land on the kicking foot.

Common Faults

- Approach isn't smooth, causing a lack of power and distance.
- Ankle isn't locked, causing the ball to be struck incorrectly.
- Last stride is too short, so the ball doesn't get enough height and distance.
- A lack of follow-through equals loss in distance of kick.

Passing with Feet

Today's modern goalkeeper must have good technical skill when using her feet to control the ball. Because of rule changes and with many teams playing flat in the back, the goalkeeper's ability to pass and serve the ball to teammates is crucial.

Key Coaching Points

- The goalkeeper should always have her entire body behind the ball when receiving a pass; there is no room for error because she is the very last line of defense.
- The goalkeeper should point to the side she wants the ball played to: either her stronger foot or her side farthest from the front of the goal.
- When asking for the ball, she should take a quick look at her options long before the pass has arrived. This gives her time to survey the field, and then she will know where she is going to distribute the ball even before she receives it.

Common Faults

- Reaching for the ball with just the foot allows room for the ball to redirect over the foot from a bad bounce or a bad trap.
- Lack of communication on the goalkeeper's part results in a pass played to the wrong foot or directly in front of the goal.
- Goalkeeper asks for the ball but does not have the appropriate time or space to receive and play without being under immediate pressure.
- Goalkeeper does not survey her options before receiving the pass, thus takes too much time once the ball is received, allowing the opponent to adjust to her next pass or tackle her.
- Not playing the simple early passes.

DISTRIBUTION DRILLS

Throwing Drill

Goalkeeper catches a cross served from one flank and immediately distributes to opposite side where an outside back is waiting to receive the throw. The distance of the defender receiving the ball can be altered; therefore, the goalkeeper has to decide if it is going to be a bowling or sling throw.

Punting/Dropkick Drill

One goal on the end line facing another goal setup on the midfield line. A goalkeeper is in each goal with ten soccer balls. One goalkeeper starts by punting or drop-kicking a ball and the object is to get it over the opposite goal. If the ball successfully goes over the opposite goal in the air, that goalkeeper gets a point. If the ball does not make it over, it is placed in the opposite goal for that goalkeeper to distribute. The goalkeeper with the most points wins. The distance of the goals can be adjusted according to ability, and the desired distance the goalkeeper should be consistently achieving. Also, restrictions can be made as to how far out the goalkeeper can punt from inside the 18-yard area.

Passing Drill

Use the same setup as the throwing drill, but now the goalkeeper is receiving a ball on the ground from the outside defender and must properly receive the ball and play it to the opposite outside defender at the right pace and distance. Two or more targets could be incorporated, and now the goalkeeper has to survey the situation before receiving the ball, and make the proper choice, to whom and when to pass the ball.

Tactics

Goalkeepers must be prepared tactically as much as the field players. It's very important that goalkeepers understand the system of play the team is using, especially in situations where planning is required. The goalkeeper is the last defender, and she must be tuned in to the team at all times. This will help reduce goal-scoring chances. When a goalkeeper is confronted with a breakaway or 1 v 1 situation, it will take both proper technique and great timing for her to prevent an opponent from scoring.

The goalkeeper must come off her line at relatively the same speed or slightly slower than the attacker who is dribbling the ball. For example, if the opponent is dribbling at a sprint, the goalkeeper must come off the line quickly and explosively. If the opponent is dribbling slowly and taking many touches, the goalkeeper must be patient and steal ground slowly. One of the worst mistakes a goalkeeper will make is to go down early for a ball because she has rushed the line. The common result is that the attacker succeeds in faking out the goalkeeper and simply dribbles around her to pass the ball into the net.

At each moment the attacker touches the ball, the goalkeeper must be in the set position, ready for a shot. Each time the ball is pushed ahead or to the side, the goalkeeper may gain ground. This produces a stop/start type of movement for the goalkeeper. The goalkeeper must be good at reading when the attacker is about to touch the ball and how far the attacker is pushing the ball ahead of her. This will allow the goalkeeper an oppor-tunity to "steal" the ball from the attacker.

There will be instances during a match where breakaways occur inside the 18-yard box; perhaps off a mis-cleared cross or corner. The goalkeeper must take into account which defenders are nearby and how to close ground on the opponent as quickly as possible. There may also be instances when smothering a volley or shot is necessary, even when a defender is pressuring the same attacker. Whatever the situation, the key moment for a goalkeeper to assess is the touch on the ball by the opponent. Players often "prep" a ball before shooting it, thus providing the perfect opportunity to pounce. On a 1 v 1 inside the 18-yard box, this "prep" moment is the time to try to smother the ball if the goalkeeper has already closed the space between herself and the opponent.

Crosses

Similar to breakaway training, crosses are all about timing and the decision to come off your line in order to successfully catch a cross, especially in traffic.

A goalkeeper must know where the ball is heading before leaving the goal line. This tends to be the biggest mistake made by goalkeepers; they start moving as the opponent is starting to strike the ball. The goalkeeper should stand her ground until she determines if the cross is inswinging or outswinging, what its height is, whether it is delivered far or near post, and how far away from the goal line the ball is traveling. Those factors cannot be determined until the ball has been struck.

Offensive Communication

Most goalkeepers think that once the ball is won, their job is complete when it comes to communication. This is an area that needs to improve, especially at the advanced levels. Goalkeepers must be educated tactically regarding defensive and offensive tactics.

These are examples of basic commands the goalkeeper should utilize in directing the players:

Step Up   The goalkeeper is telling her defenders/midfielders to push forward up the field quickly. This may be to support the counterattack or to take away the attacking space of the opponent, if possession was lost.

Turn   The goalkeeper tells her defenders and midfielders if they can turn once the ball is played into them. Outside backs, receiving a pass from their goalkeeper, will take a touch and know they have time to settle the ball and prepare it forward without pressure.

Use Me   The goalkeeper tells her teammate she is available as support, and is comfortable receiving the ball at her feet to help maintain possession or to change the point of attack.

Physical

Goalkeepers are required to have quickness, explosiveness, power, jumping ability, and agility. These are more anaerobic elements; therefore, the goalkeeper's physical training should be different than that of the field players. Pure fitness should not be ignored, but because less running is done in this position, the fitness should come from actual goalkeeping drills.

Following is a list of different physical needs for a goalkeeper and some ideas on how to train for these needs. For all of these exercises a 1:1 ratio would be adequate. This means the goalkeeper trains as long as she rests. As the goalkeeper's fitness increases, you can decrease rest and increase work time. Keep in mind, however, that a goalkeeper needs short bursts of energy. It does not make sense to work a goalkeeper for two minutes straight with a two-minute rest vs. 45 seconds of high-level work with a 45-second rest.

All the following drills are designed to improve the lateral quickness and overall reaction time of a goalkeeper. Each drill will also help increase a goalkeeper's fitness, if done using a controlled rest-period program.

Crisscross Side-to-Side   Set up 12 cones approximately six yards apart and staggered. Shuffle side-to-side between cones—no crossing legs! Explode between cones, really pushing off, 6 times.

Side-to-Side Slalom   Set up 12 cones in a straight line about two yards apart, then:

1) side-to-side slalom through, 4 times
2) two-footed slalom, 4 times
3) quickness slalom, 4 times.

Dot Drill   Cones form a square two yards apart. One whole rotation up and back counts as one. The following drill is continuous, and must be completed 30 times in a row:

1) two feet apart, two together, two apart, 6 times
2) right-leg figure eight, 6 times
3) left-leg figure eight, 6 times
4) two feet apart, two together, two apart and turn, 6 times
5) two feet apart, right foot, two apart, left foot, 6 times.

Repeat the set 4 times, trying to beat earlier times.

Square Drill   Make a square out of cones/shoes/etc. positioned two yards apart.
1) one-footed figure eights for 45 seconds, 4 times;
2) two-footed figure eights for 45 seconds, 4 times.

Two-Cone Jumps   Keep knees up to chest (if you have had knee surgery, no knees to chest but still explosive side to side); one minute, 45 seconds, 30 seconds, 15 seconds, 10 seconds, 5 seconds.

Cone Shuffles   Cones ten yards apart. Must shuffle, no crossover of feet and keep butt low. One minute equals ten times (to one cone is one, then back to next cone is two, etc.). Do four sets with 20 sit-ups in between as rest. Do sit-ups quickly!

Mirror Fakes with Partner   Two cones ten yards apart. Try and fake out a partner and race to cone. Five times and switch partners.

Straight Pressure Training and Conditioning

Each drill is done for 45 seconds to 90 seconds, depending on the condition of the goalkeeper. The rest period is equal to the time it takes to do the drill, or just alternate between goalkeepers (one rests while one works). During each time period, the working goalkeeper does as many repetitions of the movement as possible:

- Goalkeeper lies facedown. Server bounces ball hard. Working goalkeeper must get up and catch ball in the air.
- Goalkeeper squats and jumps and touches the crossbar.
- Server rolls ball out 5 to 6 feet from working goalkeeper, who dives for the ball. Ends up working in a circular motion. (This can be done for medium-ball dives, too. Server simply holds ball out at waist level and working goalkeeper dives to and takes ball out of server's hand.)
- Goalkeeper somersaults and server tosses ball (alternating sides). Goalkeeper must dive to ball.
- Goalkeeper stands with legs spread apart. Server faces with ball at feet and passes the ball through open legs. Goalkeeper must dive on the ball.
- Goalkeeper and server are 10 yards apart. Goalkeeper throws ball to server and server deflects. Goalkeeper must collect with the fewest possible bounces of the ball.
- Goalkeeper bounces ball very hard and jumps to catch, but throws it back down before it lands.
- Goalkeeper and server are 10 yards apart. Goalkeeper tosses ball directly up above head, sprints around server, and tries to catch ball before it bounces (or minimum number of bounces).
- Server stands on a bench with ball held above head. Goalkeeper jumps and grabs ball then gives it back to server.
- Goalkeeper stands on a post and must shuffle back and forth between posts 10 times, then do 20 push-ups. This is done 4 times. May change each in-between shuffle to sit-ups, knees to chest, etc.
- Goalkeeper somersaults out and server dropkicks directly at goalkeeper.
- Server is bent at the waist and holds ball in hands. Goalkeeper must leapfrog over, and turn and face server, who then throws ball to side for working goalkeeper to dive for.

13

Fitness Training

The six components of physical conditioning that need to be trained are endurance, speed, power/ strength, flexibility, agility, and coordination. No matter what component you may be training, the goal should always be the same: training the body to be able to perform and sustain effort at greater levels.

It's a given that every player must be certified by a physician as fit to take part in athletics. Then, before starting any type of conditioning program with a soccer player or team, a logical starting point must be found, to avoid injury and to test the results of the program at a later date. Once the starting point is established, it is possible to design a program to improve the levels of conditioning. The program can then be modified as the soccer player's fitness improves.

Establishing Starting Condition

The first thing to do is determine a player's maximum heart rate:

$$220 - \text{age} = \text{approximate maximum}$$

The player's heart rate is the number of beats per minute. Count number of beats for 10, 15, or 30 seconds, then multiply by 6, 4, or 2 respectively.

For example:

$$10 \text{ by } 6 = 60$$
$$15 \text{ by } 4 = 60$$
$$2 \text{ by } 30 = 60$$

The measurement can be taken by counting the pulse beats from the large artery of the wrist (radial or ulnar artery) or the neck (carotid artery).

When a player is well conditioned, her pre-exercise heart rate will be lower than that of a player who is not as well conditioned. Her post-exercise heart rate will not be as high as that of a player who is not as well conditioned. And, her heart rate during the resting period will return to normal quicker, meaning her recovery rate is shorter than a player who is not well conditioned.

Five common tests used to assess starting points:

1) Timed two-mile run, yo-yo tests — aerobic endurance
2) Six times 50-yard sprints with rest in between each sprint—anaerobic endurance
3) Sprint test—speed
4) Vertical jump and bench press —power/strength
5) 5–10–5 agility test —agility.

Common Conditioning Mistakes

- Ratio of work and rest is too long or too short, resulting in the soccer player not properly increasing her fitness base. Overtraining and possibly injury.
- The recovery period in between conditioning sessions is too short; the player's body, therefore, has no time to replenish energy stores. This, too, can lead to injury and/or less effective conditioning sessions.
- Conditioning the team as one person and not tracking individual variations. Each player will have a different fitness base, so their conditioning programs should be individualized, preventing overtraining or undertraining.
- Failure to demand proper technique when conditioning with the soccer ball. A player's skill level often decreases as she gets fatigued. It's therefore important not to reinforce bad technical habits or lack of composure just because the player is conditioning at the same time.
- Only training one component of conditioning, rather than covering all areas needed to play soccer.

- A player with an injury is trained as hard as her teammates whom are injury free. This will only delay recovery from the injury and increase the risk of further injury. In addition, because of the injury, the player will not be able to push herself as hard as her teammates, so the conditioning will not be as effective.

Notes on Conditioning

A player should be introduced to physical conditioning at different ages and stages in her career. The rule of thumb is: the younger the player, the less fitness training she should be doing. If a practice session is run properly, players under the age of 14 will get plenty of fitness just by participating in the practices and games. In addition, youthful soccer players are still in developmental stages; the time saved by excluding fitness training should be spent on training to improve their technique and skills. When training young players, one should be aware that there is a large difference in individual maturation within age groups. The growth spurt of adolescence may start as early as ten, or may not start until the age of sixteen. Coaches who coach young girls need to remember that, on average, they mature two years earlier than boys. Because of the wide range of maturation time, the coach should be careful not to discard young players based on size and strength. Care must be taken to develop soccer talents even if the players are presently physically immature.

Fitness training that might be done during a preseason session should be far different than that done during postseason play. Coaches need to understand what type of fitness is appropriate for the various stages of a soccer calendar. For example, more endurance training and lengthy fitness sessions would be used during the months building up to a season. Lighter sessions, utilizing shorter fitness tests, would be used throughout a season to maintain levels of fitness. To be safe, accurate, and successful, the coach needs to set up a yearly fitness calendar that staff and players understand and are prepared to execute.

The overall exercise intensity in women's soccer is not as high as in the male game due to the lower physical capacity of the female players. However, according to fitness researcher Dr. Jens Bangsbo, the activity profile of women soccer players is very similar to that of men soccer players, and there is little difference in the training potential of men and women; i.e., the response to training from baseline level is similar. Therefore, male and female players should basically train in the same way. Though it is important to emphasize training at a high level of intensity for women, this is known to cause changes in the menstrual cycle. The intensity of exercise, therefore, should be increased gradually, so that players' bodies have time to adjust. If a player should have menstrual changes, the player should either take a short time off, or back off from the training.

COMPONENTS OF CONDITIONING

Endurance is the ability to sustain periods of various intensities and the ability to overcome fatigue and recover rapidly. There are generally two divisions of endurance—aerobic and anaerobic—and both are very important to the soccer player.

Aerobic Training

Aerobic training can be divided into three categories: aerobic high intensity, aerobic low intensity, and recovery training.

Recovery Training

The purpose of recovery training is to aid the player in her recovery from the last game. During the game there may be small ruptures that occur to the connective tissues and muscle fibers. The damage may lead to soreness and stiffness. Through recovery training, light physical activity such as jogging or games like soccer tennis is the way to reduce the soreness and push out the lactic acid. During recovery training the intensity should be such that a player's heart rate should not rise above 65–70% of maximum range. Average: 65% of maximum heart rate. Range 40–80% maximum heart rate.

Aerobic Low-Intensity Training

The purpose of aerobic low-intensity training is to help develop a strong endurance base so the player can perform with technical proficiency at a high work rate for 90+ minutes. A top-class female player will cover 7–9 kilometers in a game.

If the coach chooses a game that is intermittent by nature, this activity must be longer than five minutes to push and maintain the heart rate. The coach needs to keep the player's heart rate at approximately 80% of maximum heart rate. Average: approximately 80% of maximum heart rate. Range: 65–90% of maximum heart rate.

Aerobic High-Intensity Training

By including aerobic high-intensity training, the coach is trying to reduce the amount of time the player needs to recover after high-intensity activity, and expand their ability to perform over long periods of time during the match. Activities should be developed that keep the heart rate about 90% of maximum for a period of approximately 5 minutes. Average: 90% of maximum heart rate. Range: 80–100% of maximum heart rate.

Anaerobic Training

Anaerobic training is divided into speed training and speed endurance. Speed endurance is needed to help the player continually produce power during the game.

During speed-endurance training practices the players will never exercise at their maximum level of intensity. But when playing it will be at their maximum, for example 2 v 2 for 1–2 minutes. Again the heart rate will be in the 80–90% of maximum range.

It should be noted that the higher the level of soccer, the more sprinting the player performs. It is recommended that this type of training should only be performed by top-class players and not by the local U-14 club team.

Interval training uses alternating periods of work and rest. Although interval training is primarily used for anaerobic-type training, there are examples of aerobic interval training.

Endurance Training Drills

Training with a Soccer Ball

Circuits Set up 8–10 different stations—juggling, heading, 1 v 1, 2 v 2, fast footwork, paired passing, shooting, trapping, plyometrics over the ball. Using the entire soccer field, position each station at equal distances and assign a number of players. Work at each station is 45 seconds in length and each rest period is one minute in length but includes the jog to the next station. This circuit can be run once or as many times as needed. This is anaerobic conditioning.

Stations Play 5 v 5. Set up a 45-by-55-yard grid with regulation goals. Two teams of five players and one goalkeeper play for five minutes. As many as four other teams are stationed at each corner of the field doing fitness with the ball. Examples given for circuit training can be used for each station and the players can rotate every 30 seconds. This is anaerobic endurance training for the players doing the circuits and aerobic endurance training for the players competing in the 5 v 5 game.

Technical Drills Any technique, such as passing and receiving, can be trained under fitnesslike conditions. The coach must set up each drill to train the actual skill and, at the same time, tax the player physically. For example, a player sits on the ground while a server throws the ball up into the air. The player must get up and control the ball with her chest before the ball hits the ground. After receiving the ball and playing it back to the server, the player must repeat the action as many times as possible in under 45 seconds. Any body part can be assigned to be used in this drill, and for various lengths of time. Another example of this type of conditioning can be done in a small group with more than one player working. The coach separates the team into groups of four or more; two rest while everyone else works. The two servers are 25 yards apart, while the other players start in the center. For one-minute intervals, the players in the middle sprint to one server and play a one-touch pass back to the server, before sprinting to the other server and repeating the skill. Any skill can also be used in this example, and the fitness can be modified by increasing/decreasing time, moving the servers closer/farther apart, and requiring the workers to jog back to the central marker after completing the skill and then sprint to the other server. This is aerobic endurance training.

Small-Sided Games Play 1 v 1 up to 3 v 3 + 1. This type of training will always focus on fitness, because it requires every player to constantly stay involved in the play. It also incorporates the tactical aspects of the game, because now the player must make decisions based on opponents and teammates. This type of training can be influenced by the size of the playing field, restrictions on touch, restrictions on numbers, goal up/goal down, length of drill, etc. Games played with only a few participants will focus on anaerobic endurance training, because the time of the games should be short in duration.

sprint-chase drill

Large-Sided Games Play 4 v 4 up to 8 v 8. This type of training will be longer in length and focus on aerobic endurance training. Again, the demands put on the players can be highly influenced by restrictions such as one touch only, and man-to-man marking vs. zoning. There should be no offsides.

Functional Tactical Training Any position on the field can be trained in this manner, and it is important that a coach does this, because each player needs to be able to perform under pressure. This pressure can be influenced by an opponent, the time given to properly execute a skill, or the various choices afforded the player being trained, and she must make the right choice. For example, the center midfielder must check back 15 yards to receive a pass from the outside back. Once the ball is received, the midfielder must turn, dribble 10 yards, and then complete a pass to one of two target players. The choice of pass depends on the pressure from an active opponent in the midfield. The player must do this ten times at game speed, then players rotate positions accordingly. This is an example of aerobic endurance training, because the player is repeating the task several times over a longer period of time.

Training without a Soccer Ball

10 by 120s The soccer player completes ten sprints of 120 yards—the time to beat is 19 seconds. The 45-second rest includes the jog back to the goal line opposite where she started. After the fourth and seventh sprint, a 90-second rest is given. This is interval training, focusing on anaerobic endurance conditioning.

Cone Monsters The soccer player completes ten shuttle sprints, always coming back to 0, proceeding out to the 25-yard marker. The time to beat is 35 seconds, and the same amount of rest is awarded after each series is completed. After the fourth and seventh sprint, the rest time is doubled. This is interval training, focusing on anaerobic endurance conditioning.

Strikers The soccer player sprints 40 yards out and back three times under 50 seconds. A 45-second rest is given between sprints. This exercise is repeated eight times. This is interval training, focusing on anaerobic endurance conditioning.

Sprint/Chase Soccer player A sprints to the 15-yard marker and sprints back to the starting cone. As soon as player A takes her first step to sprint to the 30-yard marker, player B sprints to the 15-yard marker, while trying to beat player A to the marker. Player A completes the sprint by reaching the 30-yard marker and then sprinting to the starting point. The drill is continuous until each player has completed the series ten times. Each team has eight players, so while three are working, five are resting.

Cooper Test   The soccer player must try to complete two miles in 12 minutes. The average adult female soccer player can reach $7^1/4$ laps on a regulation track when match fit. This is an example of aerobic endurance conditioning.

Gauntlet   The soccer player runs one mile proceeded by a one-minute rest, a half mile proceeded by a one-minute rest, and then 400 yards; i.e., the goal is to run a 6:15-minute mile or better, a 3:30 half mile or better, and a 1:45 lap or better. The most efficient way to organize this fitness session is to partner-up players. One runs the test while the other keeps track of work times and rest times. This is an example of interval training, focusing on aerobic endurance conditioning.

Yo-Yo Intermittent Endurance Test   This test consists of 5–20-second intervals of running interspersed with regular, short rest periods (5–15 seconds). The test evaluates an individual's ability to repeatedly perform intervals over a prolonged period of time. The test is great for soccer players, because soccer is an interval sport.

Power/Strength

The ability to overcome and/or counteract resistance though muscle activity calls for a combination of power and strength. Without enough power-energy in the muscles being used, a soccer player cannot effectively perform the common tasks needed in a 90-minute game (jumping, kicking, tackling, passing, dribbling). In addition, she will be highly susceptible to becoming more seriously injured, more frequently.

All female players competing on the college level and in advanced competitive arenas should be on some type of weight training program. Power can be developed through playing the game of soccer; however, incorporating a weight training regimen with soccer training it becomes much more advantageous for the player. Such programs can vary according to the time of year and the level of power a player already has before weights lifting. Each athlete is different; therefore each weight training program should be catered to the individual's specific needs. Each player should be tested in specific types of lift or strengthening activities in order to find out where she should start in terms of weight percentage and repetitions.

Weight Training Programs

In the off-season, the program is to focus on building up power and strength, making gains in areas of weakness. During the last few months prior to the season, the strengthening program should be tapered to just maintain the gains that have been made. When the season arrives, the program is again adjusted to focus on injury prevention and game preparation. Lighter weights and more reps are used during the season vs. heavier weights and less repetitions in the off-season.

When attempting to get on a weight training program, seek the advice and guidance of a professional strength/conditioning coach. Some types of lift commonly seen in a female soccer player's weight training program include but are not limited to squats, leg presses, step-ups on boxes at various heights, lunges, bench press, shoulder press, pull-ups, and sit-ups. Regardless of the type of strengthening exercise in the program, the common thread is the muscles must be warmed and stretched before weight training. A player does not want to lose flexibility from lifting, and well-developed muscles are not detrimental to good flexibility as long as muscle-building training is combined with flexibility training.

Soccer-Specific Power Exercises

- All running/jumping exercises where body weight is used for resistance (jumping rope, hopping on one leg, running uphill or up stairs).
- Plyometric training can be done for both strength and speed. Again, these are exercises using the body weight as resistance, where the player bounds and leaps at various distances, heights, repetitions, and time duration. As a player's strength increases, these factors can be increased.
- Push-pull exercises with a partner, can be done with or without a ball.
- All running exercises will help increase the power in the legs to a certain degree.
- All soccer-related games from 1 v 1 to 11 v 11. The smaller-sided games are more taxing on the body and legs, so should be shorter in length.

Flexibility

Flexibility is the ability to use the joints and muscles to perform such tasks as planting and turning, and kicking the ball. Flexibility is the full range of motion about the joint. Agility is coordination.

Factors Affecting Flexibility

Muscles Good flexibility is not hindered because of muscle mass unless strength training is not combined with flexibility training. Muscle tone can also affect the flexibility; if a muscle suddenly tightens because of fatigue it will lose flexibility.

Temperature Flexibility in the muscle will increase as temperature increases. This is why it is so important to have an active warm-up before a game. Also, if it's cold out, players should dress in proper gear, e.g., wearing sweat tops and bottoms, while warming up will help increase flexibility.

Joints The structure of joints is biological and cannot be changed by training for soccer; however, the flexibility of joints can be affected by the ligaments and tendons surrounding the joints. These can be improved with proper training.

Flexibility Training

Active Stretching The player swings and bounces, moving the legs or arms as far as the joints and muscles will allow. This type of stretching, e.g., jogging across the field and raising one leg then rotating outward to stretch the leg muscles and the hip joint, isn't constant but it happens during a game and will increase active flexibility.

Passive Stretching The player remains stationary while stretching certain muscle groups and joints.

Partner stretching can be incorporated to help increase flexibility; however, the partner needs to be focused on her teammate in order to prevent overstretching and injury. When a player is stretching a particular muscle and joint, she should isolate this area so it is not contracting. Also, a player should stretch each muscle for a count of 10–20 seconds, relax for a few seconds, and then stretch the same muscle again to increase the effectiveness of the stretch.

Speed

Speed in soccer is the ability to carry through on a thought or a task as quickly as possible. There are several types of speed skill that soccer players must develop and be able to perform throughout a game:

Psychological Speed The ability to speedily recognize game situations as they are occurring and successfully predict what an opponent, based on behavior, is about to do. This recognition speed often comes from a player's level of experience and can only be trained-in through consistently playing the game itself.

Speed of Action How quickly the body reacts to the recognition/anticipation of the game situation.

Technical Speed How quickly a player is able to maneuver the ball at her feet: dribbling, receiving, passing.

Pure Speed The ability to cover the distance between two points.

One can only improve pure speed by a measure of three to ten percent. Although this percentage is small, even the slightest increase in a player's speed can make a big difference in the overall outcome of a game. At the highest levels of competitive soccer, the speed of play is extremely fast, and one must be physically and mentally able to perform in such an environment.

During speed training the player should perform maximally for a short period of time (less than ten seconds). The rest periods should be long enough for the muscles to recover to near resting condition, so the player can perform maximally in the next exercise. Speed training has to be performed at the early stages in training, when the players are not tired. A good key for recovery time is five times the exercise duration. Depending on the number of repetitions, speed training can be very time consuming.

Whenever possible, speed training should look like the game of soccer; it should be functional. This will improve the player's ability to anticipate and react to different situations. When speed training soccer players, the coach should stay away from formal speed training signals; for example, a whistle as a start command for sprinting over a set distance. A whistle in soccer means stop. Soccer players respond to visual cues. Signals in soccer would be a moving ball or the movement of a teammate or opponent. Duration 2–10 minutes. Rest 5 times the exercise time (for example, 5 minutes time × 5 = 25 minutes rest). The intensity is 100%, repetitions 2–10 as determined by the coach.

Speed-Training Practice

Relays Separate the team into as many equal teams as needed; e.g., five teams of five. Set up a marker 15 feet away; each team has one ball and the first person in line must dribble to the 15-foot marker and sprint back without the ball. The second player must sprint to the marker and dribble the ball back. The third player must do as the first, and so on (speed of action/speed of changing direction). Three times each.

Sprints Players practice in groups of four.

Practice 1 In turn, one performs a sprint while the others rest and stretch. The sprinting player starts by taking the starting position, on one knee. At a signal (ball drop, hand goes up in air), she sprints to the marker which is 15–20 yards away. Her "rest" includes the jog back to the group and then some stretches. The sprints are done five times for each player, and the start position can vary—on both knees, lying on stomach, lying on back (speed of action).

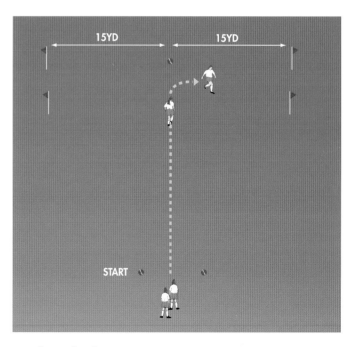

speed practice 1

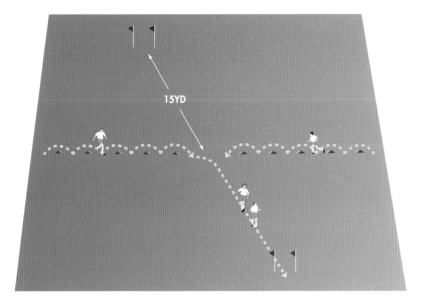

speed practice 3

Practice 2   One player jogs from start to marker; partner follows two yards behind. Leader sprints to either gate, partner reacts to give chase. Variations: Partner sprints to opposite gate; leader can "go" from anywhere along the midline.

Practice 3   With ten cones set up as shown across the field, players approach each other, synchronizing their jumps to land together. Leader goes for either gate. Defender reacts and chases. At next stage, defender reacts to leader's move by racing to opposite gate.

Practice 4   Players jog into shaded zone. Leader turns and sprints for line B or sprints forward to line A. Defender reacts and gives chase to the line.

Box Run   15-yard-square grid, two teams on opposite corners. The first person on each team sprints around the square trying to catch the other. The drill is continuous until one team catches the other. The size of the square can be increased or decreased to change the work ratio. Also, teams can be made smaller, which will decrease the rest ratio. This is an example of interval training focusing on anaerobic endurance conditioning. Change directions intermittently.

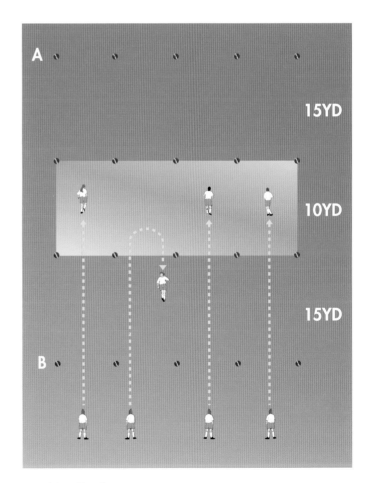

speed practice 4

Lap Ahead   Player A starts at the very back of the group of players already one complete lap ahead of the group. The group of players must run around the designated area (e.g., half a soccer field), and try to catch player A as she continues to jog/run around the designated area. This exercise can be dictated by how fast player A runs around the outside of the area. This is an example of aerobic endurance conditioning.

Sectionals   Set up various coned sections around a designated area (e.g., half a soccer field), and color code each coned section. When a player is running towards a yellow cone it is a sprint, a red cone a jog, a blue cone a walk, a pink cone a backward sprint. The length between cones can vary, as well as how many cones of each color and what they designate. This is an example of fartlek running, which is frequent changes in speed over various distances throughout a predetermined run. It is also an example of anaerobic or aerobic endurance conditioning, depending on how long and how intense the run will be.

Goal Posts   Two groups, one in the center circle resting, the other working. The group working must run around the goal and back around the other goal and finish in the center circle where they started. One time is given for the entire group and is determined by when the last person in the group enters the center circle. The other group must now beat this time while the group that just ran rests in the center circle. The distance of the goals depends on how far you want the players to run (e.g., full field, top of each 18-yard box). The rest should be active.

Agility

Agility is the ability to combine quickness and coordination while executing technical skills with the movement of the feet and the body when reacting in gamelike situations. Players with great agility

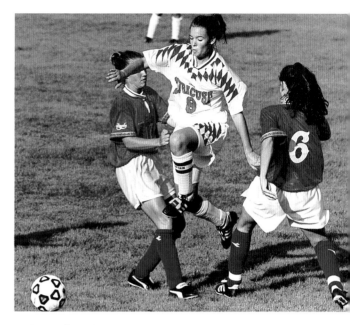

agility to "ride" tackles

can be more effective when dribbling in tight spaces and under pressure, often avoiding hard tackles. In addition, it helps in defending, because an agile player can quickly react to a change in ball direction or when marking an opponent. Agility can be trained using various drills without a soccer ball or with a soccer ball. Agility can be incorporated in practices to make sessions more skill-related.

Agility-Training Exercises

Triangle Drill   The player sprints backward from cone 1 to cone 2, then sprints from cone 2 to 3, backpedals from 3 to 4, and then finishes with a sprint to cone 2. The player does this five times and then switches direction around the triangle and again goes five times. A one-minute break is given between each run.

Cone Hops   The player hops over a cone four times and then sprints for 10 yards. This is done five times starting on both sides of the cone. Then the player hops front/back over a cone four times, then sprints forward 10 yards. This is done five

cone hops

times, starting both in the front and the back of the cone. A soccer ball can be used as the cone, and when the sprint is done the player must dribble the ball while sprinting.

Star Drill   The player starts by shuffling, back pedaling, or sprinting to the center cone and then to cone 1. Then she jogs back to the start and repeats the same process all the way around through cone 8. One rotation can be one set, and three sets can be done doing different footwork training or even using a ball. Also, the player could start from different body positions; such as lying on the back, lying on the stomach, kneeling.

T-Dribble   The player starts at the top of the "T" and must move the ball in and out of the cones as quickly as possible using all parts of both feet. Restrictions can be made to force the player to use only certain parts of the feet when dribbling, and the space can be made tighter to further test a player's agility.

Balance/Coordination

Balance and coordination allow a player to adjust and handle soccer specific situations with speed, accuracy, and success. For example, while a player is dribbling down the field, she is suddenly confronted by an opponent who attempts a tackle but fouls her instead. Using good coordination, the player will more than likely roll out of the tackle and save herself from injury or, by using a sudden change of direction or quick moves with the ball, she can "ride" the bad tackle and continue down the field.

Coordination is influenced by several factors: speed of action, speed of reaction, endurance, power. All of these components are needed in a combined effort to develop well-coordinated moves on the soccer field. A player may recognize what to do in a situation, but if she does not have the speed of action and is lacking endurance near the end of a game, her coordination will be affected negatively.

push-pull drill

Direction

A player needs to know where to go when reacting to someone else on the field or a situation. For example, a goalkeeper must react to a cross in the box while being pressured from an opponent on one side when trying to catch the ball.

Timing

The sense of timing is a must for good coordination and often times is influenced by a player's experience level. If a player is given enough opportunities to head a ball served into the penalty area, then eventually she will be able to successfully judge the distance, speed, and timing of the serve when attempting to head the cross.

Technical Skills

When a player has been taught proper technique in the various skills used for playing soccer (passing, receiving, heading, tackling, shooting), coordination can be enhanced. At the same time, good coordination is needed in order to obtain solid technical skills. It's therefore important to have a natural level of coordination that will allow for the training of technical skills. Once these skills are mastered, coordination is increased in pressure situations. For example: a player practices receiving balls with her back to the goal and turning under

no pressure before shooting into the net. Now a goalkeeper is added, and the player still must turn and accurately shoot the ball into the net. Next a defender is added, who tries to keep the player from turning and/or tries to intercept the ball.

Coordination Training Exercises

- In push-pull games with/without a ball, players have to react to loss of balance and adjust weight and body in order not to fall and to protect the ball. Also, if players do fall, they should roll out of their fall, rather than just stop on the ground.
- Play a version of team handball where the players can only pass with their hands but must score off their head. Put restrictions on the game, such as: players can only take three steps with the ball in hand, can have physical contact on a player with the ball but no fouling.
- During one small-sided game, enlarge the playing area and then reduce the playing area. The players will have to adjust to tighter spaces and more contact vs. larger spaces and more room to run.
- Goalkeeper throws a ball in the air, rolls forward and must catch the ball before it hits the ground. Field player throws the ball in the air, rolls forward, and must trap the ball with any body part before it hits the ground.

- Doing sprints through flags, slalom run side to side. Player must be carrying ball in hands at same time and pass it off to next player in line when the sprint is complete.
- All practices under pressure—1 v 1, 2 v 1, 3 v 2.
- Ball-juggling during rest period while doing interval training. The player is fatigued, but must have good concentration and technical skill to keep ball in the air.

In fitness training, a coach who decides that the players aren't getting what they need out of it needs to monitor and change the intensity of the exercise. Here are some ways for a coach to change training intensity:

- Change the rules.
- Vary players: adjust number/majority vs. minority.
- Set limitations: e.g., three touches only.
- Use balls: assign one per player per group, set number of touches per.
- Vary goals: number/location/size.
- Use various-sized field areas.
- Institute consequences: i.e., winning vs. losing.

Warm-Ups before Training

In planning warm-ups, the coach must keep in mind the aims of a proper warm-up: to improve performance and to decrease the chance of injury.

During the long season, the burden is on the coach both to change the warm-up periodically and to be somewhat creative. With top-class players, the coach needs to remember that the motivation is the ball and the game; so to achieve an effective warm-up, the coach needs to use the ball as much as possible to motivate the team.

To help avoid the risk of training injury, the coach should make sure that the warm-up takes in all of the large muscle groups used in the game. This can be done by playing some type of passive game.

paired stretching

Pregame Warm-Up

After warming up before a game, the biggest physiological concern is the loss of the muscle temperature generated by the exercise, before the game actually starts. If the break before the game is less than five minutes, a player can quickly regenerate that warmed-up muscle temperature. However, if the break is longer, players need to start the warm-up over.

Coaches need to be aware of the psychological value of a warm-up to players. There should be some time allocated for the player to do "her own thing" outside of the group warm-up. In soccer, some of this warm-up needs to be with the ball so the player has some type of "touch" on the ball before the kick off.

Next, be sure that players warm up again as halftime ends. It's been shown that the running distances of players starting the second half is shorter than those in the first half. One possible reason is that the players are cold, physically, in the second half—perhaps even mentally, since many goals are scored in the first five minutes after halftime.

Glossary

active rest   easy activity designed to simply keep a player "warm"

at speed   full speed

breakaway   rapidly moving forward into space

chip   short, lofted pass from foot jabbed sharply underneath the ball

cross   service from the flank area by the attacking team into the opponent's penalty box

cutback   reverse movement to gain space

dribbling   maneuvering the ball with touches

"dummy" the ball   allow the ball to continue forward without touching it, while pretending to touch or receive it; let it continue on to a teammate

fartlek running   interval training (sprinting l0 yards, jogging l0 yards, sprinting 10 yards, and so on...) over a prescribed route or distance.

first touch   first contact as ball is received

flick   light redirecting header

front third   attacking third of the field

free kick   a penalty kick awarded to fouled team

half volley   full kick of ball upon ground contact

heading   striking the ball with the forehead

high pressing   immediately attempting to win possession of the ball once it is lost

knees up   knees tucked to torso prior to plyometric jumps

knockdown   redirection of ball to the ground

lofted pass   soft, short, high pass

marking   man-to-man coverage, or 1 v 1

pace   speed; as in, to take pace off the ball

pass   movement of a ball over a distance

play on the break   counterattack

playmaker   player designated for highlighting; i.e., "making the play"

plyometrics   exercises designed to train explosiveness of the lower body, often repeated a certain number of times or over a specific distance (for example, bounding or jumping for height over 30 yards, hopping back and forth over a "pony" on one or both legs)

pony   hands-and-knees position

push pass   pass using inside of foot

receiving   controlling incoming ball

save   a goal prevented

service   a pass of the ball

shielding   using body to protect possession while on attack

show   indicate readiness to receive

shuffle   move while still maintaining ground contact

smother   covering ball with body

space   open area to which to move or play

"square/flat"   defending player in a straight-line position

stroke   light "control" touch on ball

swerve pass   pass that "bends" around defender

sweeper   free player behind defender; helps organize the defense while picking up loose opponents or passes in defensive and midfield thirds

tackle   direct regain of ball possession

volley   full kick of in-flight ball

wall   barrier of players' bodies

"with the laces"   using the instep

yo-yo tests   testing, developed by scientific researcher Dr. Jens Bangsbo of Denmark, which focuses on aspects of physical conditioning and helps determine the fitness level of soccer players before, during, and after training

About the Authors

Robert "Butch" Lauffer is one of a new generation of young soccer coaches who grew up playing the game of soccer in the United States and abroad.

Beginning at the age of seven, he progressed to the North Texas Soccer Association U-19 State Team in 1979 and 1980. As a player with the famed Texas Longhorns Soccer Club in Dallas, Texas, he took part in 110 international games for the club, playing and traveling in Mexico and throughout most of Europe. He also played in tournaments such as the Gothia Club (twice), the Helsinki Cup, and the Munich Cup, a tremendous upset because this was the first United States team to win a major European tournament. Later, he coached and traveled with the Texas Longhorns U-12, U-14, and U-16 teams to England and Scotland, all by the age of 20.

Mr. Lauffer attended the Carnegie School of Physical Education and Human Movement in Leeds, England, from 1981 to 1983, and was there selected Player of the Year in 1983. He returned to the United States and received a B.S. in Kinesiology from Texas Christian University, where he was also captain of the soccer team in 1984. He also received his masters degree in 1988 from Texas Christian University after serving as the Graduate Assistant Coach to both the Men's and Women's Division I Soccer Programs.

He has worked with the North Texas Soccer Association, with the training and selection of players for the state team, as well as conducting coaching licensing courses. He was Staff Coach for the United States Youth Soccer Association in 1987 for Region 3, a National Team Administrator for the United States Soccer Federation U-16 National Team Tour of Scotland in 1988, the USSF U-20 National Team trip to Las Cruces for the Interregional Tournament in 1988, and the Men's NCAA National Tournament in 1997, and he is currently a USSF National Staff Coach. He holds an "A" license, the Irish Football Association Full Badge, the National Soccer Coaches Association of America Advanced National Diploma, the English Football Association Preparatory Course preliminary badge, the United European Football Association "A" License (1998) and the U.E.F.A. Professional License (2000). He is the author of *Coaching Soccer* and *Soccer Coach's Guide to Practices, Drills & Skill Training*, published by Sterling.

He is currently Head Coach of Men's/Women's Soccer at West Texas A&M University in Canyon, Texas.

April Kater was born in Summit, New Jersey, and attended the University of Massachusetts. As a player, she won the title of Soccer America Freshman of the Year in 1987 and was from 1988 through 1990 an NSCAA First Team All-America, and a two-time Adidas First Team Academic All-America. In 1990 she closed her collegiate career by being named the top female soccer player in North America, receiving the Herman Award.

Ms. Kater participated in three Olympic Sports Festival events and was a member of the National "B" team throughout the early 90's. Returning to her alma mater after serving as a Graduate Assistant Coach at West Virginia Wesleyan College (1991–1993), she helped coach U. Mass. to the 1993 NCAA Final Four and 1994 NCAA Tournament.

In the summer of 1995, she was appointed to the first head coaching position of the women's soccer program at Syracuse University, Syracuse, New York. In its first four seasons under Coach Kater, the NCAA Division I Women's Soccer Team has compiled 50 wins/24 losses/4 draws, and reached the second round of the NCAA Tournament in 1998.

As a regional coach for the East Olympic Development Program, she worked with the U-14 age group (1998) and the U-17 age group (1999), and was a regional team coach for the U-19 age group (2000). For the past five years, Ms. Kater has been the director of the Syracuse Girls' Soccer Camp, opening up the sport of soccer to girls and young women.

Coach April Kater is a member of the United States Soccer Federation and the National Soccer Coaches Association of America. She holds a NSCAA Premiere Coaching Certificate and a USSF "A" Coaching License.

Index